Captain Cohonny

Constantine Maguire, *c.*1830

Captain Cohonny

Constantine Maguire
of Tempo
1777—1834

W.A. MAGUIRE

THE BELFAST SOCIETY
IN ASSOCIATION WITH
THE ULSTER HISTORICAL FOUNDATION

For Joanna

First published 2002
by the Belfast Society, c/o the Linen Hall Library,
17 Donegall Square North, Belfast BT1 5GD
in association with the Ulster Historical Foundation
12 College Square East, Belfast BT1 6DD

Distributed by the Ulster Historical Foundation

© W.A. Maguire
ISBN 0-9539604-5-5

Printed by ColourBooks Ltd
Design and production by Dunbar Design

Mrs Hawkins and John James, by Thomas Lawrence, 1805.
Lord Abercorn paid £50 for this superb portrait of his favourite mistress and
their son (b. 1800, d. 1808). When exhibited at the Royal Academy in 1806
it was entitled 'A Fancy Group'; it was not seen again in public until 1894.

CONTENTS

LIST OF ILLUSTRATIONS

ACKNOWLEDGEMENTS

For permission to use and quote from essential sources in their care, or of which they own the copyright, I thank the Deputy Keeper of the Records, the Public Record Office of Northern Ireland, the Duke of Abercorn and Sir James Langham, Bt; likewise the directors of the Public Record Office in London, of the City of Westminster Archives, of the National Archives in Dublin and the National Library of Ireland. The staff of all these institutions – along with those of the Linen Hall Library, Belfast, Queen's University Library and Enniskillen Branch Library – greatly facilitated my research.

I wish also to thank some of the individuals who have particularly helped this little book on its way, namely Deirdre Crone, Pauline Dickson, Elizabeth McCrum, Trevor Parkhill and Tom Wylie; Professor Desmond Greer; Drs D.W. Harkness, A.P.W. Malcomson and W.E. Vaughan; Gerry Healey, Margaret Kane and Michael Smallman; Catherine Blumsom, Joanna Gault, John McCabe and Justin Martin; Jean Farrelly, Heather McClean and David Ronan. Charles Robert Maguire and Michael Martin generously shared with me their material on the Tempo Maguires. Valerie Wallace's shrewd comments made me think twice (and change my mind more than once) about the fascinating Frances Hawkins/Maguire.

The sources of the illustrations, where relevant, are acknowledged in the accompanying captions. I am especially obliged to the Duke of Abercorn for his kindness in letting me use the portrait of Mrs Hawkins by Lawrence, and to Terence Maguire (The Maguire of Fermanagh) for permission to reproduce the portrait of Constantine Maguire.

INTRODUCTION

ONE MORNING EARLY in the month of May – the opening line of many a popular ballad – in the year 1793, a young man named Thomas Russell set out from his sister's house near Kesh in County Fermanagh to walk all the way to Belfast, a distance of nearly a hundred miles. Russell was the boon companion and friend of Theobald Wolfe Tone, a lively Dublin lawyer. Both were leading figures in the Society of United Irishmen, a radical club recently established in Belfast and Dublin. Russell thought nothing of such a journey on foot. Besides, for all that he was a gentlemen and former Army officer, he was so poor that he could not afford to travel by any other means. His route took him through Tempo, a small village on the road between Enniskillen and Fivemiletown (which, as one may guess, was five miles from nowhere in particular). Tuesday 7 May that year was a beautiful spring day, so, when he reached Tempo, Russell paused for a while to admire the view. As was his habit, he took out the pocketbook he always carried and jotted down a few notes in his almost unreadable scrawl. This is what he wrote:

> Set out on foot by way of Tempo. Over the mountains. The way lonely and wild which I like … Maguire of Tempo a Protestant. Conform'd. His ancestors were lords of all this country [Fermanagh]. He has about 2000£ p. annum. A pretty place. A glen with a stream and growing woods. The place I now write in is a field. A river running close by me. The hills, except where I am, rise out of the water. Cover[ed] with the stubble of old wood. Firrs [furze, gorse] in bloom. Primroses and a lofty bridge thro' which is seen the same. No sound but the gentle noise of the water – calm, serene and dark. An angler far up.[1]

Ten years later, released from prison, where since 1798 he had been

confined without trial as a dangerous radical, Russell took part in
Emmet's rising of 1803, was caught and hanged in Downpatrick for
treason. All that was in the future, but even in 1793 he was well aware
of the power of the conservative forces that opposed the ideas and
ideals of United Irishmen such as himself. Nowhere in the north of
Ireland was it more evident than in Fermanagh. The gentry of the
county, he wrote in his journal, were all 'horrible torys'. Radicals
found it difficult to organise there, the more so because Presbyterians
(who were attracted to radicalism more than most other religious
groups) were comparatively few in Fermanagh. Catholics, who were
numerous, were mostly indifferent if not downright hostile to the
French revolutionary ideas so admired by the United Irishmen. In
any case, they lacked leadership, their natural leaders – the Catholic
gentry – having faded away. Well before 1700 the Maguires of
Tempo, who, as Russell noted, subsequently conformed to the
established church, were the only remaining gaelic and Catholic
landowners left in the county.

The owner of Tempo at the time of Russell's visit was Hugh
Maguire (c. 1750–1800). By all accounts the name given to an earlier
Maguire, Hugh the Hospitable, would have been apt for him too, for
he entertained in lavish style. In fact he lived well beyond his means
and by the time he died in 1800 had been forced to sell all but a
fraction of the estate. The purchaser of the last major portion, a linen
merchant from County Derry named Lyle, sold it in turn to a Belfast
banker, William Tennent. He did so with evident regret, writing to
Tennent about the place in words that confirm the impression it had
made on Russell twenty years earlier:

> Now that I am speaking of the Demesne, it is one of the most
> beautiful spots you ever saw, wood and water delightfully disposed
> and in the very heart of the estate; if it had been possible for me to
> leave the County of Derry I would have gone there to live. You may
> have a dish of fish out of the river every day of the year, plenty of
> crawfish in the river, also plenty of game, in short I think the
> Demesne would give a family everything but wine and groceries ... [2]

As it happened, Tennent in his younger days was well acquainted with
Thomas Russell: both of them in the 1790s were members of the
Belfast Society of United Irishmen, and they were fellow prisoners in
Fort George in Scotland between 1799 and 1802.

Hugh Maguire had three sons – Constantine, Brian and Stephen – the first of whom is the subject of this book. Young Constantine was evidently a rebellious and hot-headed youth. There is no evidence that he and Russell ever met, but he appears to have been sympathetic to the ideas of the United Irishmen. At any rate, in 1798, when the unrest that had been simmering in many parts of the country broke out into armed rebellion in some counties, Constantine and his brothers were involved in a fracas with the Church of Ireland curate of Tempo in which shots were fired. Prosecuted by the enraged clergyman, the three were indicted by the grand jury at the Enniskillen Assizes and sent for trial. Charges of assault against the two younger boys were withdrawn, but Constantine was tried on the far more serious charge of firing with intent to kill and was found guilty. Amazingly, he escaped in that hanging year with a sentence of three months in prison and a fine of £50. The members of the grand jury – Protestant landowners who clearly believed that sinister political motives must have lain behind such an attack on a clergyman of the established church – entered a furious protest in their record book with the words: 'He ought to be hanged'.[3]

The sentence of the Enniskillen court is confirmed in print in the report of the Inspector-General of Prisons, which appears as an appendix to the Irish House of Commons journal. Curiously, though, Constantine's crime is there described simply as 'An Offence'. Presumably he was confined in the old gaol in Enniskillen, which was described in the inspector's reports at the time as 'very old, inconvenient and insecure … for the most part covered with timber, an extremely dangerous roof'. Given the damp climate in Fermanagh and an almost total absence of heating (the local inspector, on one winter visit, found all the inmates huddled round the only fire in the building, with the gaoler's wife presiding), it was also an unhealthy place.

Later in the same year, the *Belfast News Letter* printed part of a letter reporting a rebellion scare in Enniskillen: 'We were greatly alarmed here on Monday last. The gates of the town were shut, and upwards of seventy persons arrested here and in the surrounding country. I understand there are examinations lodged against 62 of the persons in custody …'. No names are mentioned but – plausibly enough for a known troublemaker and recent gaolbird – Constantine is said to have been among those arrested. These people were not riffraff: the report tells us that most of them were 'respectable people, four of them Doctors of Physic'.[4] According to John O'Donovan, a noted Irish scholar who worked in Fermanagh for the Ordnance Survey in the 1830s and visited Tempo then, the Maguire boys had been brought up wild; their indulgent father was said to have been amused when Constantine and Brian practised their marksmanship by shooting apples off each other's heads with pistols.[5]

William Tennent was to become an important figure in Constantine's life. The loss of his childhood paradise, and his attempts over a period of many years to regain it by buying it back or leasing it from Tennent, forms one important strand in the career of 'Captain Cohonny' (as Irish-speaking tenants around Tempo called him). Another, closely intertwined with the first, concerns his marriage to a famous beauty, their bitter quarrel and the mistress who replaced her in his affections. A third strand follows the tortuous route by which he arrived in Tipperary and deals with his awful death there. These themes help to illuminate some obscure corners of the history of the period, and occasionally touch on larger matters. Their common core is the raffish gentility of the man himself and his curious story, a story that rivalled – if it did not surpass – anything in fiction.

Seal of Constantine Maguire (enlarged)
DRAWN BY DEIRDRE CRONE

Constantine Maguire's signature

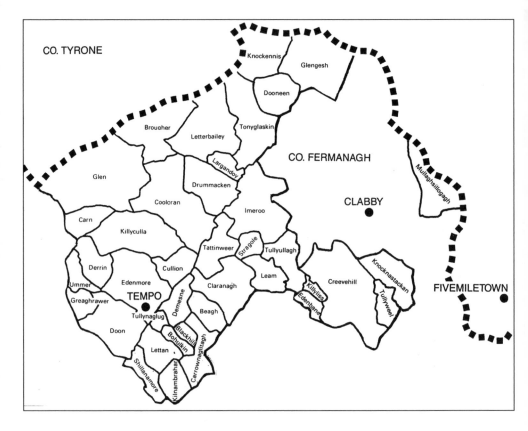

The lands of the Maguires of Tempo
(in modern townlands), *c.* 1760

REDRAWN BY DEIRDRE CRONE

1

THE MAGUIRES
OF TEMPO

CONSTANTINE MAGUIRE was born about 1777. His father, Hugh, was the only son of Philip Maguire, fourth son of Brian (died 1712), whose father Cúchonnacht had been killed at Aughrim in 1691 fighting for King James II. The Tempo estate had then been confiscated by the victorious Williamites and granted to a Protestant, but Brian successfully appealed for its restoration on the grounds that his father had only had a life interest in the property. By 1702 the family was back in possession. Brian restored its fortunes by marrying Bridget Nugent, from Coolamber, County Longford, whose father – like his own – had been a colonel in the Jacobite army and who brought with her a large dowry. When Brian died suddenly in his mid-thirties, Bridget Maguire turned Protestant in order to safeguard the inheritance of her four sons, three of whom subsequently converted when the need arose.[6]

The Tempo estate was created in the reign of James I as part of the plantation of Ulster, during which several branches of the Maguire family had been given grants of land in Fermanagh – formerly called Maguire's Country. The first of them to settle at Tempo, Brian (died 1655), had somehow managed to hold on to all his property, even under Cromwell, whereas his kinsmen lost theirs by taking part in successive, unsuccessful rebellions. His own son, who had taken the side of the rebels, was killed in battle in 1650, leaving an infant heir named Cúchonnacht, the casualty at Aughrim mentioned above. In modern terms the property in the seventeenth century consisted of 13,000 or more acres in the barony of Tirkennedy and another 2,000 or so in south Fermanagh, in the barony of Clanawley. The size of the

'The Old House at Tempo in 1853' from a watercolour sketch
in the Emerson-Tennent Papers

PRONI

estate was somewhat reduced in the last quarter of the century, when
young Cúchonnacht Maguire came of age and began to live well
above his income; he was also at the cost of raising and equipping the
regiment of infantry he led at Aughrim. Further reductions took place
during the eighteenth century, but the property inherited in the
1770s by Hugh Maguire was still a substantial one, and his financial
position was further improved by the fact that he was sole heir not
only of his father Philip but also of his uncles Hugh (died 1766) and
Robert (1778). His marriage in 1773 to Phoebe Macnamara, daughter of a respectable family of similar status to his own in the west of
Ireland, set the seal on his apparent good fortune.

There was, however, a long-looming cloud on the horizon. His
uncle Hugh – in his twenties a captain of grenadiers in the Imperial
service, later lieutenant-colonel of a regiment in the British Army –
had married in 1745, as her fourth husband, the immensely wealthy
English widow of a Scottish general. Lady Cathcart, as she continued
to be called after she became the Colonel's lady, was considerably
older than her Irish husband. Once married, he became a domestic
tyrant and, when she refused to give him all the money he demand-
ed, carried her off to Ireland, to a house in Fermanagh not far from
Clones. Using her money, he not only paid off the debts on the
Tempo estate but also bought out his mother's relatives in order to
acquire Castle Nugent in Longford. Selling the Fermanagh property,

he moved to Longford and set up as squire. There, when she proved obstinate about handing over her jewels and the title deeds of her manor in Hertfordshire, he locked up his wife in the attic, where she remained in solitary confinement for a dozen years or more. She was released, almost out of her wits, only when he died in 1766 (of lock-jaw, the result of a knife wound sustained during his search for the hidden title deeds). Amazingly, Lady Cathcart recovered from her ordeal and lived to be ninety-six. As soon as she had her wits and her lawyers about her, she sued her late husband's representatives – ultimately his nephew and heir Hugh – for her share of the money he had used for the benefit of himself and his relatives. Negotiations dragged on for years, without much success for the vengeful widow in her own lifetime. Ten years after her death in 1789, however, her executors eventually succeeded in forcing the sale of most of the Tempo estate in order to settle the accumulated debt – hence the much-diminished inheritance to which Constantine Maguire succeeded in 1800. The story of Lady Cathcart's dreadful experience first became generally known in polite circles through a lengthy obituary in the pages of the *Gentleman's Magazine.* Later, it was used by the novelist Maria Edgeworth, who also knew about the goings-on at Castle Nugent more directly through her father (whose estate at Edgeworthstown was only a few miles from the place), as the basis for the story of Sir Kit Rackrent in *Castle Rackrent* (1800). The real wicked colonel thus achieved lasting fame as a character in fiction.

We know almost nothing about Constantine Maguire's upbringing except O'Donovan's story about the William Tell antics of himself and his brother Brian. That tale is plausible enough in a general way, for the late eighteenth century was the golden age of duelling in Ireland, when 'fire-eaters' such as Fighting Fitzgerald abounded; Sir Jonah Barrington, a leading exponent of this illegal activity himself, despite being a judge, remarks in his memoirs that in some parts of the country the only questions a father ever asked about a prospective son-in-law were 'What's his family?' and 'Did he ever blaze?' Not only that, the tradition of military service in foreign armies was no less strong among the Maguires of Tempo and their relatives than among other Catholic gentry. Constantine's great-uncle Hugh had been preceded in foreign service by two of his own uncles on his father's side and by four on his mother's. There is also some evidence that Constantine's father Hugh may have served in Europe before returning home to become head of his house and name; at any rate he is referred to as 'Captain' by O'Donovan.

Inevitably, adopting the language, religion and culture of the Protestant landowning class diluted the 'Irishness' of the old Irish gentry. Cúchonnacht ('hound of Connacht') as a male forename (one would hardly call it a Christian name) was replaced in documents and other official references by Constantine, which was a different name rather than an English equivalent. Constantine remained Cúchonnacht to his Irish-speaking tenantry at Tempo, however, and was generally known there as 'Captain Cohonny'. The Tempo Maguires are a good example of the hidden strains and subterfuges in such families, because we have access to evidence from Vatican sources which reveals that fact. Outwardly at least Hugh Maguire conformed to the established church, performing his duty as a Protestant like his neighbours, all of whom were Protestant. Indeed he must have made a convincing show of it, for when the development of Tempo in the late 1700s prompted the vestry of Enniskillen to abandon the old thatched church at Pubble for that part of the parish and build a new one in the village, Maguire not only gave the land but had a pew set aside in the building for himself and his family. At any rate, Hugh Maguire must have had the confidence of his fellow landowners when chosen in 1780 as high sheriff of the county – an appointment open only to Anglicans.

Nevertheless, he did not intend to give up the ancient right of his family to nominate the clergy of the Catholic parish of Enniskillen, namely a parish priest for Enniskillen and a curate for Tempo. We owe our knowledge of the matter, as so often, to a dispute that created a document.[7] This row began in 1793, when the parish priest of Enniskillen died. The Catholic bishop of Clogher, Hugh O'Reilly, forestalled the traditional procedure by appointing his own man instead of one or other of the two suitable nominees put forward by Hugh Maguire's devoutly Catholic eldest daughter. Maguire protested and appealed the case to Rome, where his cause was promoted by a kinsman, Denis Maguire, bishop of Kilmore. Denis Maguire's agent in Rome was Fr James Cowan, OFM, guardian of St Isidore's College. At the bishop's request, Fr Cowan prepared a manuscript in Italian – discovered a few years ago in the Franciscan archives in Killiney, Co. Dublin – which was the basis of Maguire's appeal to the cardinals. This summarised the case as seen from Tempo.

Bishop O'Reilly had apparently rejected the nomination of the Cavalier Maguire, as the manuscript calls him, on two grounds – first, that he was unable to prove his right by the production of suitable documents and, second, that being a Protestant he had forfeited any claim to exercise it. Maguire's reply to the first was that his family had exercised the right as far back as anyone could remember, which was manifestly the case. Given the disturbed history of Ireland, there was scarcely a Catholic family that could produce original documents, yet others had not lost their rights on that account. Reference was made to Cúchonnacht Maguire's martyrdom at the battle of Aughrim, and to the actions of his descendants who had sustained the faith in difficult times and had built new Catholic churches in the parish.

As for the bishop of Clogher's second point – that Hugh Maguire was a Protestant – his daughter who had made the nominations was a devout Catholic. The bishop simply ignored this fact. 'The father of this lady', he wrote, 'is one who turns away from the true doctrine, a pervert [a theological term for someone who knows the right but chooses to deny it] and a putative protestant'. Fr Cowan's memorandum conceded that heretics and schismatics who sought to destroy the church and educated their children to take the same view ought to be excluded from the right of presentation, 'but our Cavalier', he wrote,

> is a very long way from being one of them. He is solely a protestant in name. He is not a protestant through hatred or malice but solely of necessity. The Cavalier is seen between two extremes, i.e. either to make an external act of conformity with the false protestant religion, or to see himself flung headlong downwards from the summit of grandeur to the bottom of the abyss of poverty, misery and mendicity. Between these extremes he had not the courage to embrace the heroic part.

Furthermore, we are told, Hugh Maguire's wife Phoebe was a practising Catholic, their children were brought up in the faith, the local curate said mass in the manor house every Sunday and feast day, and the whole family received communion twice a year. All this, it was pointed out, was a great deal more favourable than in the case of Lord Clanrickarde a few years earlier. In that instance, Rome had upheld Clanrickarde's right of presentation to the parish of Loughrea, Co. Galway, when the person nominating, his sister Letitia Moore, was the only Catholic in the whole family.

The dispute over Enniskillen dragged on for several years. The authorities in Rome referred it back to Ireland. Meantime, the Maguires had added a third name to their list, a move which evidently strengthened their hand. Edward Kernan, recently ordained at Salamanca, was to become an important figure in Fermanagh, both in religion and politics. Bishop O'Reilly's nominee apparently continued in post at Enniskillen, but only on a temporary basis as administrator of the vacant parish. Kernan was installed as parish priest in 1799. As bishop of Clogher himself in the 1820s, he was to turn up again in the story of the Cavalier Maguire's son Constantine.

The truth of the matter seems to have been that Hugh Maguire's daughters were indeed raised as Catholics but the boys passed as Protestants. He himself was thoroughly pragmatic, if not indifferent – an attitude apparently inherited by his sons. There is no doubt, however, about the family's sympathy for Catholic concerns. The pretensions of a Catholic bishop were an altogether different matter, in which family pride took precedence over theology. On the whole the outcome of the dispute with Bishop O'Reilly was a victory for Hugh Maguire. Almost immediately, however, this triumph was overtaken by the event that was to ruin Maguire himself and to shape his family's future, namely Lady Cathcart's posthumous success at law and the sale of most of the Tempo estate. In the longer term the game was lost not so much by religious indifference or neglect, still less by the bishop's machiavellian manoeuvres, as by the diminished status of the head of the family and his disappearance as a familiar presence in Fermanagh.

2

MILITARY
MANOEUVRES

Oof them. For his eldest son, Constantine, he purchased a commission
in the Army as an ensign (the most junior of infantry officers, little
more than an apprentice soldier) in the 27th Regiment of Foot in
February 1799. Two months later, in April, Constantine became a
lieutenant, again by purchase, in the 88th Foot (the Connaught
Rangers).[8] After serving in Flanders, in a shambles of a campaign in
which the British commander, the Duke of York, became a byword
for marching his men aimlessly up and down, part of the regiment
had seen hard service in Grenada and St Lucia and had to be re-
formed, a process that was carried out in Jersey early in 1799, when
Constantine transferred to it. Later in that year it embarked for India,
reaching Bombay early in 1800. Thereafter it spent some time in
Ceylon waiting for transport to Java. Instead of proceeding, however,
it was included in the Indian army under the command of General
David Baird sent to Egypt to help clear the French forces stranded
there after Nelson's victory at the battle of the Nile.[9]

Baird's army, made up of British regiments and sepoys, sailed for
Egypt at the end of December 1800. Baird's intention was to land at
Suez, at the head of the Red Sea, where his presence would divert
some of the French defending Cairo and Alexandria. The passage
from India was slow, however, and the fleet was then prevented from
reaching Suez by monsoon storms. In the end, after months of delay,
the army landed on the Egyptian coast at Cossir in June. Intrepid as
always, Baird resolved to march across the desert to the River Nile. In

the height of summer, despite night marches, the troops suffered terribly from heat and thirst (made worse by bad water and dysentery and scarcely helped by a daily ration of a pint of cheap wine per man for the Europeans). Many died, but the bulk of the force of 7,000 reached the river in August. Ordered to proceed to Cairo, Baird conveyed his troops downriver in boats, a lengthy operation. He did not meet the commanding general until 1 September, by which time the French in Cairo had capitulated on terms. Alexandria, where the remainder of the French were holding out hoping for reinforcements from Europe, capitulated shortly after. Baird's army had arrived too late, except to help police the evacuation of the defeated enemy.

Though the expedition was, like so many combined operations far from home and at the mercy of weather and vague strategy, a fairly comprehensive fiasco, the sheer guts displayed by Baird and his men in their epic journey across the desert caught the popular imagination in Great Britain. When the general returned home, briefly, after twenty years of continuous service in the Far East, he was hailed as a hero and knighted by the king.

In 1802, when the Peace of Amiens brought fighting between France and the United Kingdom to a temporary halt, the 88th returned to England, where it was reduced in strength. Constantine was among the officers put on half pay. When hostilities resumed in 1803, however, he did not return to active service, probably because his health had suffered from the privations of the campaign. Many years later, when answering a War Office questionnaire in 1828 as to the willingness of officers on half pay to serve again if required, he wrote that he was 'afflicted with Sciatica and other severe Rheumatic affections caught while in the East Indies and Egypt ...'. Instead of rejoining his regiment in 1803, he was given a staff appointment in Ireland as an adjutant in the Recruiting Department. Such work, however essential it was to the success of the long war against Napoleon, can scarcely have given much satisfaction to an ambitious and impoverished young officer. During the years 1803–07 Lieutenant Maguire was attached to the Belfast recruiting district, which covered the north of Ireland. In August 1807, when that appointment ended, there was a mysterious episode in his military career. The bare fact of it was recorded in the 1828 questionnaire, where he noted that on 13 August he was placed in the 9th Foot (a rather good regiment) for forty-three days but thereafter was continued on the Recruiting staff; 'his appointment to the 9th Reg. having been cancelled' is the only explanation given. Did his health let him down? Was he for some reason unacceptable to his fellow officers? We simply do not know. What we do know is that from October 1807 to October 1816, when he was reduced to half pay again (for the rest of his life, as it turned out), Captain Maguire was adjutant of the Athlone recruiting district. In 1828 he described himself as 'one of the oldest Staff Adjutants in the United Kingdom'. At that time he had served seventeen years on full pay and nearly thirteen on half pay. Feeling himself to be 'unfit for active service, and having been promised', he hoped 'soon to be appointed to the first vacant District in Ireland'.[10] Such hopes were quite unrealistic, of course: the Recruiting Department was not itself recruiting, and he was by contemporary standards too old to be seriously considered for any vacancy.

Constantine's brothers also had military careers of a sort. Brian was nominated to a commission in a sepoy regiment of the East India Company's army at Bombay. We know much more about Brian's adventures in India than about those of Constantine, because Brian not only became notorious but on returning to Ireland published his memoirs.[11] Though probably a work of fiction in some respects, and certainly in places inaccurate as history, the *Memoirs* are both entertaining and also of some interest as evidence of assumptions and attitudes among Irish gentry of native stock who had conformed in religion but had retained a strong sense of national feeling. Published in Dublin in 1811, four years after his return to Ireland, this pamphlet of sixty pages deals first with setting the record straight about the hero's adventures in India, where his military career ended in his being cashiered for duelling, imprisoned and sent home in disgrace. It is prefaced by an 'Advertisement' stating that 'his object only is to rescue himself and a respectable Irish family from the malignity of cowards, and the calumnies of the envious' (news of his doings had apparently spread from the Indian papers, whose 'studied odium' had been 'copied into those of Europe, particularly in Ireland', to the distress of his family). His time in India was spent at Bombay, Cochin and Surat, where he 'passed several years undistinguished by any occurrence but such as are incidental to a military life; marches and counter-marches – skirmishes – taking and relieving forts...'. At Cochin (formerly Dutch) he was attacked in a tavern (kept by a Frenchman who had been one of Hoche's soldiers in the attempted invasion of Ireland in 1796) by an American sea captain who detested the occupying British soldiers almost as much as the Dutch did. Defending himself with only a billiard cue against a drawn sword, Maguire cracked the skull of his adversary, who died a few weeks later.

Obliged to leave Cochin, the intrepid Maguire then survived a hair-raising voyage in an open boat, outwitting a band of pirates en route. 'That damn'd thing called honour', however, apparently the prevailing interest of his life, led in 1806 to his downfall in Bombay, after several comparatively quiet years when he killed nobody worth mentioning. Banished, on the way home he spent some time on the island of St Helena, where he was imprisoned again after becoming involved in a fracas with twenty-three drunken officers who tried to exclude him from a public room in a tavern. He shot one of them and routed the rest. A jury acquitted him of blame, but the governor of the island confiscated his guns and put him on the next ship for England. In London, 'while waiting for a remittance from his family' – a not uncommon state of affairs – he had several more encounters. More still were to take place in Dublin, where he eventually settled (an inappropriate term for what followed). The *Memoirs* end with a fanciful genealogy of the Maguires which traces their descent from AD 175 and ends with the author's own marriage in December 1808. According to one source, copies of the *Memoirs* were bought up by the author's friends and relatives in order to withdraw as many as possible from circulation. It is certainly hard to find a copy, so perhaps they did not spend their half-crowns in vain.

After his return to Ireland, Brian Maguire was frequently in trouble (and in the newspapers) over his forceful advocacy of the cause of Catholic emancipation. He seems to have made it the pretext for some of the many public brawls for which he became notorious in Dublin. Most people went out of their way to avoid him, for his intimidating manner and eccentric appearance were frightening, till he met more than his match in the person of a theatrical performer named Bradbury, who gave him a tremendous public beating. Less was heard of him thereafter – in Dublin at any rate – until the mid-1820s, when he was tried (and acquitted) on a capital charge for accidentally beheading an old woman in the Wicklow Mountains with a ball from a twelve-pounder cannon he had set up to protect himself from arrest by the authorities. Such bizarre Hibernian behaviour was later, when his elder brother was murdered, to provide colourful background copy for press reports, in both English and local papers (the *Clonmel Herald* of 22 November 1834 copied an item from the *London Standard*). There is one other possible sighting of this dangerous eccentric in his prime. A contemporary ballad, quoted by W.C. Trimble in his *History of Enniskillen*, names a Captain Brian Maguire as the organiser and leader of the Catholic party in an affray known as the Ashwoods Fight, which took place in December 1823 near Enniskillen. Though one cannot be certain (the encounter was not reported in the local press, presumably because no one was actually killed), it is not unlikely that 'the Ribbonmen of Castlecoole and likewise Beggar-street' were led on this occasion by an ex-officer of sepoys.

Hugh Maguire's youngest son, Stephen, does not appear to have been provided for by his father at all. After Hugh's death in 1800, the boy's mother and eldest brother had him entered at the King's Inns in Dublin as an apprentice attorney. Curiously, his educational background is recorded in the entry books as an academy in Islington – presumably a crammer's. These efforts to equip Stephen with a profession soon proved to be vain. Enlisting as a common soldier, he disappeared from view and was never heard of again.

Of the five sisters, Frances and Elizabeth did not marry and were still living with their mother in the 1820s. A third, Maria, made an exotic match, marrying the Marchese de Zigno Patavino, an Italian nobleman from the Austrian-ruled north. One of the genealogical documents relating to the Maguires of Tempo, now in the National Library in Dublin, was compiled in order to prove her right to sixteen heraldic quarterings – essential for gaining entry to the court of the emperor in Vienna.[12] Fortunately, her grandmother's Butler relations and her great-grandmother's Nugent and Talbot connections made this condition easy enough to meet. We have no idea how Maria met her husband, but all three of these families, like her own, had long-established links with military circles on the Continent and, in an age of patronage, kinsfolk knew their duty. Her brother Constantine had a similar document prepared and authenticated by the Herald's office in Dublin in 1830, to prove that he was chief of his name and descended from the same ancestor as Alexander Maguire, last claimant to the title of Lord Enniskillen, who had died unmarried and without issue in France in 1801. Alexander had been a captain in Buckley's regiment of the Irish Brigade.

3

MARRIAGE

A TALE OF TWO MISTRESSES

DEPRIVED OF MOST OF HIS PATRIMONY by his father's extravagance and Lady Cathcart's posthumous triumph, Captain Maguire (to give him his usual title) had difficulty in making ends meet. His army pay was small, while his income from the remnant of the Tempo estate – nominally just under £350 a year – was subject to an annuity payable to his mother and, because of the number of long leases with years still to run, unlikely to rise much in the near future. These circumstances did not permit a young officer to cut much of a dash, except perhaps temporarily by raising loans on the security of the property. The payments to his mother soon became irregular. Eventually she was obliged to sue him in the court of Chancery in Dublin for the money owing to her. What any prudent gentleman in Constantine's position needed was a good wife with a large fortune. Instead, he married Mrs Hawkins.

Frances Augusta Hawkins, born Maclean, was a Scotswoman of good family, a sister or half-sister of General Sir Fitzroy Maclean, 8th Baronet. Who Hawkins was, and why and when she married him, is a mystery, like the rest of her early life (there is no sign of her birth in the available Maclean genealogies), but she was known by his name when she came to public notice as the mistress of John James Hamilton, 9th Earl and 1st Marquess of Abercorn (1756–1818), sometime in the 1790s. Abercorn inherited titles in the peerages of three kingdoms – Scotland (Earl of Abercorn and Baron Paisley), Ireland (Baron Mountcastle and Viscount Strabane) and Great Britain (Viscount Hamilton) – when he succeeded his uncle in 1789; a year later he was created Marquess of Abercorn in the peerage of

Ireland.[13] Along with these dignities came great wealth from estates in Ireland and Scotland (where substantial houses were maintained at Baronscourt in County Tyrone and at Duddingston near Edinburgh). He himself in 1788 had purchased Bentley Priory, at Stanmore in Middlesex, which he was to make his chief residence, and there was also a town house in Grosvenor Square; in both of these he entertained royally (and royalty) for many years. Not content with all this, he pursued a claim to a dukedom in France that an ancestor had once held. Furthermore, as Romney's portrait of him shows, he was a strikingly handsome young man, athletic in figure, graceful in manner and distinguished in appearance – not, as one critic remarked, to be mistaken for an ordinary man.[14]

He certainly did not want anyone to make such a mistake, and became notorious for his stiff manners, 'Castilian pomp' ('Don Magnifico' was one of several similar nicknames) and proud demeanour. His eccentricities became more marked as he got older; he wore the blue ribbon of a Knight of the Garter even when out shooting, and the housemaids had to wear white kid gloves when making his bed. Fear of catching from servants the tuberculosis that ravaged his family may have been the rational explanation of the latter oddity. He was remarkable too (and much remarked upon) for the boldness and frequency of his amorous affairs, pleasing himself in his choice of both wives and mistresses. His first wife, the daughter of a mere baronet, whom he married in 1779 died in 1791. Less than six months later – a scandalously short time – he married his own cousin, Lady Cecil Hamilton, his uncle's fifth and youngest daughter, whom he had managed to have promoted to the dignity of an earl's daughter through his influence with the prime minister, his friend William Pitt the Younger. Since her four elder sisters were leapfrogged in the course of this unprecedented manoeuvre, gossip strongly suspected that Lady Cecil, who was the widow of a man named Copley, had become Abercorn's mistress while his first wife was still living. As it turned out, the second marriage foundered. Lady Abercorn having fallen in love with a Guards officer and eloped with him, Abercorn was obliged to divorce her in 1799. A year later, he married another widow, Lady Anne Hatton, whose reputation was not entirely spotless. Lady Holland, who professed herself scandalised by Abercorn's choice, confided to her diary that the new marchioness had had several well-known liaisons: 'Lord A. is a man capable of doing anything, whatever outrage it may be upon decency, to obtain a woman he likes…'. As for the bride, she added: 'If she closes her amorous career with one of the greatest matches in the Kingdom, I don't know how young women will credit wise precepts of "Virtue alone is rewarded, etc. etc."'[15]

At the time of the marriage, Frances Hawkins had been Abercorn's acknowledged mistress for several years. The only clue we have as to how this came about is a remark made by her counsel in a matrimonial lawsuit many years later. 'This Lady', said the barrister, 'who is most highly respectable by birth and connexions, had unfortunately by a most singular and deplorable combination of unfortunate circumstances, fallen in early youth. She had fallen, however, into generous hands …', namely those of 'a Nobleman now no more' (Abercorn died in 1818).[16] At the height of the affair, Abercorn set up his mistress in a fine house in Beaumont Street, Piccadilly. By the time of his third marriage, in 1800, when he was living more at the Priory, Mrs Hawkins was established nearby, just across the park. Gossip reported that Lady Anne was obliged to be civil to her rival; she was even said to have conveyed her husband to his mistress's door on occasion. Given the notorious formality with which the Abercorns conducted their matrimonial relations, this is perhaps doubtful, but the only surviving letter to Abercorn from Frances ('Fan') includes the sentence, 'I am going to write to Lady A.', so there was civility at least. During her reign as his official mistress Frances gave birth to several children of Abercorn's. The favourite child was John James Hamilton or Fitzjames, born in 1800. He and an older sister are mentioned in the letter from Frances to her lover just referred to, which was apparently preserved only because Abercorn used the back of it to scribble notes for a speech on. Undated but probably about 1804, it goes as follows:

> Dearest J.J.
>
> I looked out for you yesterday, but saw you not!! Polly is at home. I had a letter from her this morning. I have been quite idle and good-for-nothing these two days, and of course the hours hang heavy, which they generally do when J.J. is not looked for.
>
> I hear dear Lord Hamilton [Abercorn's son and heir by his first wife; died 1814] is almost well. No news. Expect a long list of complaints from little J.J. We are all very naughty! Little girl [probably

their daughter Hariot] plagues my life about her lessons. I have sworn this day to give up all further annoyance to her or myself.

I am going to write to Lady A.

God bless you, best and dearest J.J. Ever your affectionate and grateful Fan.[17]

The relationship between Abercorn and Frances was clearly an affectionate one: anyone who knew him would have been amazed that she could dare to address him so informally. Characteristically, Abercorn defied convention – defied all decency, some of his critics said – by commissioning a picture of Frances and young J.J. from the most fashionable portrait painter of the time, Thomas Lawrence R.A. (later Sir Thomas and president of the Academy) and exhibiting it publicly in the Academy's 1806 exhibition. There are a number of references to the picture, and to the reactions of those who viewed it, in the diary of Joseph Farington, an influential member of the Academy whose opinion Lawrence sought in the course of painting it. The first sight of it was noted in Farington's diary for 12 February 1805 – 'Went to Lawrence as he wished to have my opinion upon the Circular picture which He was painting of Mrs Hawkins and John James Hamilton, a son of Lord Abercorn'. He next noted, under 29 April, the glowing opinion of the painting expressed by his fellow artist Fuseli, who had seen it the day before. Such a picture, Fuseli told him, 'had not been painted these 100 years ... Sir Joshua Reynolds could not have done it ... it was singly worth all the pictures Gainsborough had ever painted ... it exhibited the most exquisite ideas of pleasure without exciting any vicious feelings ... he would, if he could, give ... 2000 guineas for the gratification of possessing it...'.

In May 1806 Farington was accompanied to the Exhibition by a more critical Academician, James Northcote. In Northcote's opinion, though the picture showed a great deal of practical ability, 'it wanted breadth and repose; the Colours striving against each other'. His main objection, however, was on moral grounds: 'The Woman looks like a *Whore*, which was not necessary as she might have been made to appear jocund without it'. What was worse, Lawrence 'had infused a similar expression into the countenance of the Boy, which at least, for his age, was unnatural. He looked as if he had been bred among the vices of an impure house'.[18]

When the boy died suddenly in 1808, aged only eight, Abercorn and Frances were stricken with grief. Abercorn had his remains buried in the Hamilton family's vault at Stanmore, and erected a memorial to him in the grounds of the Priory. The inscription runs as follows:

> In the Garden which, having been a scene of amusement to six other beloved Children, had just been dedicated to the amusement of John James Hamilton, this stone is dedicated to his Memory. He was a sweet and promising Child! Born, on an inauspicious day of the Year 1800, in 1808, on 29 April ... he died! Happy for himself! For he had not yet committed Fault or felt Unkindness or known Misfortune: but to the bitter Anguish of his surviving parents.[19]

Long before their favourite boy's death, the affair between his parents had begun to cool. In the summer of 1803 Frances accompanied the Abercorns to Ireland to visit the Marquess's estate in County Tyrone. She did not stay in the house but in the Lodge, where she remained for some weeks after the Abercorns left early in September with their princely entourage to visit the estates in Scotland and so back to London – a progress that took a whole month. At Baronscourt, meanwhile, Frances exercised her undoubted charms on every man she came across. The agent in Strabane, James Hamilton junior, a bachelor, was particularly susceptible, so much so that someone must have informed his master, for on 24 September he wrote to Abercorn to confess that he had become 'insensibly ensnared at the Lodge', having passed 'some most delightful days' there, accompanied by his brother Stewart Hamilton, rector of Strabane. 'Upon the fullest consideration of the subject', he concluded, and 'well weighing every circumstance, it seems to be thought most advisable for me to endeavour to forget what has passed. When we parted with her this morning it seemed to be her intention of setting off for England on Tuesday'. He could not help adding: 'Go when she may it is impossible that any one (for so short a stay) could have left behind a greater number of people truly sorrowful at her departure.' And then, 'I feel myself a good deal relieved by the declaration I have (not without much difficulty) brought myself to make. May I presume to entreat that you Lordship will not mention the matter to any person else...'.[20]

Back at Stanmore, Frances corresponded with James Hamilton from time to time during the next couple of years. Hamilton was evidently a reluctant letter-writer, for in January 1805 he reported to Abercorn that he owed Mrs Hawkins two letters. By that time her hold on Abercorn had weakened. Farington noted in his diary for 2 September 1805: 'Mrs Hawkins is to go to Ireland, and thereby remove a cause of jealousy in Lord Abercorn's family'. The move took some time to arrange, however; she did not arrive at Baronscourt until the spring of 1806. Frequent references thereafter in the correspondence of Abercorn's agent and employees show that she was quite at her ease as chatelaine of the place. Letters from John James Burgoyne, at that time the farm manager (he later succeeded Hamilton as agent, and was for many years provost of Strabane), who was as charmed by her as every other man, mention some extravagant housekeeping: she laid in eight hundredweight of soap, supplemented a couple of months later by another half-ton; a new roof she wanted for the Lodge was estimated at 60 or 70 guineas; she ordered 200 gallons of whiskey, some of which was given out to a body of Yeomen under Lord Mountjoy (another victim of her charms) who had paraded before her at Baronscourt; and she sent a coach and horses, along with her maid, to Dublin to fetch her daughter home from school. James Hamilton began to haunt the place again. Once again, someone wrote anonymously to Abercorn, this time accusing the agent of drunkenness and neglect of duty. The wretched man had to admit he had dined with Mrs Hawkins 'perhaps 4 or 5 times or maybe oftener'. Meanwhile, she was becoming more and more an object of scandalous interest and gossip among the plain folk of Tyrone. By May 1807 she was heavily pregnant. On 17 May, Burgoyne reported an unpleasant incident:

> On Friday Mrs Hawkins was out boating and during the time she was passing up and down the lakes the labourers rested on their spades to stir [stare] at her. Being reproved by Wm Duncan they said ... that there was sufficient work in the country and that they could earn as good wages elsewhere. I considered it best, by Mrs Hawkins' approbation, to dismiss them.[21]

In fact, by that time Mrs Hawkins was Mrs Hawkins no longer. On 1 June 1807 James Hamilton wrote to tell Abercorn that he had just spent five days at Baronscourt, where he had met Captain Maguire.

Maguire had told him 'for the first time' of his marriage to Mrs Hawkins, 'which had long since taken place, and privately'. Hamilton went on to explain the curious events that followed:

> He [Maguire] expressed a wish that the form should again be solemnised by Stewart [the Rev. Stewart Hamilton], which was accordingly done that evening in presence only of Miss Croke and I. This however is a secret, and the former marriage is the only one known or spoken of.

He then added: 'In the course of the night Mrs Maguire was safely delivered of a fine boy, and she is as well as could possibly be expected'.[22] However secret Maguire's wedding may have been, it was no secret that he himself was not the father of this child. Abercorn had visited Baronscourt in September 1806, just nine months before the birth. Since the marchioness did not accompany him to Ireland on this occasion, he was free to enjoy a last fling with his mistress before bringing their liaison to an end. He evidently made it clear to her that she would be free to find someone else, whether husband or lover, and would be generously provided for.

He was back in Ireland in the late summer of 1807 for a long visit, accompanied this time by his wife and family. The coming of age of his son and heir was celebrated in great style at Baronscourt in October. The whole party – an impressive entourage – set out for London by way of Scotland early in December.

We do not know exactly how or when Constantine and Frances first met, but, quartered not far away in Derry, a bachelor officer was likely sooner or later to come across the famously beautiful, flirtatious and sociable Mrs Hawkins. We do know, from James Hamilton's letters to Abercorn, that Maguire (who had been ill) spent Christmas 1806 convalescing at Baronscourt; and, from a different source, that he was accompanied on that occasion by one of his sisters, also named Frances. The marriage of his mistress to Maguire must have been solved a problem for Abercorn. Some years earlier, in 1800, he had settled on her an annuity of £200. This sum was doubled later to £400, a substantial pension and scrupulously paid by both himself and his successor. Apart from her other charms, with £400 a year she must have appeared a good catch to an impoverished young soldier. As her barrister was to remark many years later, when the two of them faced each other in court, 'In fact there can be no doubt whatsoever that, in addition to the personal attractions of this Lady (and attractions she certainly possessed in no ordinary degree)... this annuity of £400. formed no trifling ingredient in the resolution of the Subaltern in a regiment in country quarters ... to enter into this marriage'.[23]

Apart from the note quoted earlier, Abercorn's correspondence with his now ex-mistress does not survive, but it is clear from the letters of James Hamilton that the marriage was actively approved by his employer. During the next few weeks, Hamilton reported accompanying Maguire around the area in search of a suitable home; on 14 June he had been for three days 'riding the county [Tyrone] with Captain Maguire in search of a house with about 20 acres of land'; when nothing suitable could be found locally they looked farther afield, towards Letterkenny in Donegal. 'Your Lordship may rely on it, I shall not fail in showing them every attention in my power', Hamilton wrote, adding 'I have invited them to spend some days at our house'. Abercorn evidently made it clear that Mrs Maguire was the one whose interests were to be chiefly considered, for Hamilton's reply to his (missing) letter includes the significant sentence: 'I perfectly understand your Lordship's distinction between Mr. and Mrs. Maguire, and I will take good care to act agreeably to your Lordship's wishes'.[24] If Constantine had hopes of immediately making free with his wife's fortune he may well have been disappointed, for the terms of the annuity specified that the money was to be for her sole and separate use and benefit, free from the 'control, debts and engagement of any Husband whom she should marry'. If there were any inducements other than an alluring wife with money of her own and a powerful potential patron, they left no trace in the Abercorn records. At the end of July 1807, Hamilton's news was that Mrs Maguire had rented a house in Derry, while her husband was in Dublin pursuing his military career. The outcome was the curious episode mentioned earlier, when he was briefly placed in the 9th Foot only to be returned to Recruiting, followed by the transfer of himself and his new family to Athlone. Given her hitherto luxurious style of life and extravagant habits, Frances must have found a provincial garrison town in the Irish midlands a rude shock, both culturally and socially. Matrimonial relations appear to have been normal, however, for a few years at least. There were several children. Only one survived, a daughter named Florence, born in Athlone in 1809. According to that informative barrister already quoted, there was no evidence of any more after 1810.

We know nothing at first hand about their feelings for each other during the next few years, but the marriage began to fall apart. The Maguires were apparently living in Dublin in 1813 when a girl named Eleanor Gavan (or Gavin) became friendly with Frances and a frequent visitor to the house. Constantine allegedly seduced Ellen Gavan under his own roof and they became lovers. Ellen's father found out about the affair when his daughter became pregnant in 1814. He promptly brought a suit for damages, and Constantine had to buy him off. This was how Frances discovered her husband's adultery. He wrote to her confessing his guilt, asking (after a fashion) for her forgiveness and begging her not to be too hard on the wretched girl. As a good example of his insinuating style, the letter is worth quoting at length:

> It is needless to enter into the feelings with which I address you on the present distracting subject; suffice it to say, poor Ellen is far advanced in a state of pregnancy, and having nothing but my honour to depend on, I must make her all the reparation in my power. For all this you are alone indebted to yourself, for I most solemnly swear by every power of heaven and earth she never should have fallen by me so long as she continued to visit at my house. She will ere long be lost to society, and I shudder to think of it. Though fallen, she is yet proud and virtuous. I have no female friend to whose care I could confide her till her accouchment takes place, and your ready acquiescence to meet my wishes is all the consolation I have. I little thought I should ever have such a crime to answer for – a crime rendered greater by the prior and subsequent circumstances attending it. Let me beseech you never to let an illnatured word escape your lips respecting poor Ellen, for, in the act of her fall *I* only am to blame. Do not either be premature in mentioning her name to any – you ought, and I think will feel for me. The state of my mind is dreadful. Her worthless father has just been made acquainted with it, but he shall not treat her ill. I can say no more – you can imagine the rest – Adieu!
>
> Your letter I have got safe, and will attend to all you say … I never knew what such a crime was, and trust I never will again; neither did I ever feel so severely the want of a friend. She, poor soul, is all but dead.[25]

Constantine appears to be denying that the seduction had taken place while Ellen was under his roof, and to blame his wife for expelling the girl when her suspicions were aroused and thus forcing them into each other's arms somewhere else. At the same time, Frances appears to have agreed to help the unfortunate girl, presumably on the understanding that the affair was at an end and would not be repeated. Appeased, Frances condoned her husband's misconduct, only to find that the affair was soon resumed.

Actions speak louder than words. In 1816 Constantine attempted to annul his marriage. The state of the law relating to marriage at that time, whereby the slightest hint of technical irregularity in the ceremony made it easy – indeed scandalously easy – to find cause for annulment, ought to have given him a good chance of success. He was thwarted, despite some underhand work on his part, by Abercorn. Frances had appealed to her former protector, who had turned the matter over to Burgoyne, James Hamilton's successor as agent. The pretext for challenging the validity of the marriage was that the ceremony performed at Baronscourt in 1807 had never been officially registered. On 24 July 1816, Burgoyne wrote to tell Abercorn of the steps he had taken:

> Immediately on receipt of your Lordship's letter I went to Mr. Colhoun [a local lawyer] and got him to go to Mr. Stewart Hamilton [rector of Strabane], as if commissioned by Mrs. Maguire to demand the certificate of her marriage. Mr. Hamilton declared that he had sent it twice on former application, but supposed his letters had been intercepted by Mr. Maguire.

From what we know of Constantine, this was a fair guess. Burgoyne then relayed Colhoun's opinion that a marriage carried out by a clergyman of the established church under licence did not need to have been registered: 'In England he says there is a law making it necessary but none here...'. Burgoyne added, 'I most sincerely feel for Mrs. Maguire, and trust in God she may obtain justice'. He then obtained a declaration from Hamilton, who had performed the ceremony, proving the fact of the marriage. A copy of this was sent to a barrister named Deering, who gave his 'decided opinion in favour of the legality of Mrs. Maguire's marriage' but advised that it ought to be registered all the same. 'This I immediately enclosed to Mrs. Maguire', wrote the agent on 2 August, 'and hope to meet Mr Deering at Omagh, where he can draw up the legal form of a

21

certificate to be signed by Mr. Hamilton'. Towards the end of September he was able to report success: 'I was in Derry on Wednesday last and got every entry and certificate fully settled for Mrs. Maguire, whose mind will I trust be now set forever at ease...'. Faced with this legal firepower, Constantine gave up his attempt to end his marriage in order to marry his mistress. Three months later, Burgoyne made a final comment about the affair:

> I was extremely happy to have it in my power to be of service to Mrs. Maguire, both as it was your Lordship's wish, and as some return for her former friendship towards myself. Fortunately I succeeded in getting everything she wished done.

A year later, Burgoyne provided a glimpse of the Maguire marriage as seen by an outsider, in a letter dated 22 July 1817:

> When I was in Dublin I called to see Mrs. Maguire. She was extremely anxious to sell some of Arrowsmith's maps, as I believe from pure want of money, Mr. Maguire having spent all she had, and left her to shift for herself.[26]

In practice, it would appear, it had proved impossible to prevent the husband from plundering the wife's resources.

4

MORE WORK
FOR THE LAWYERS

'The letter of the law' is no empty phrase. There is nothing like lit-
igation for generating written records. If it were not for the law-
suits in which he became involved we should have scarcely any
original material about Constantine Maguire. As it is, there are some
court records and – more valuable still for what they reveal about the
man himself – some of the letters he wrote in the course of these dis-
putes or correspondence about him from other parties concerned in
them. For the ten years or so from 1814 to 1824 – a crucial period in
his life – we rely on two such sources: the correspondence of the
Belfast banker William Tennent, who in 1814 bought from Samuel
Lyle the estate at Tempo that Lyle had purchased from Constantine's
father; and a pamphlet, published in Dublin in 1833, entitled *A
Report of the Proceedings in the Consistorial Court, Dublin ... in a Suit
for Divorce and Alimony, instituted by Mrs Frances Augusta Maguire,
against Constantine Maguire, Esq. for adultery, &c.* The author of the
pamphlet was Mrs Maguire's counsel in that suit, Dr Thomas Wallace
KC, whose speech on her behalf included transcriptions of a dozen letters, now long lost, from Constantine to Frances, as well as useful
information about both parties.

The two important points to note about the Tempo lands are these:
first that the property sold by Hugh Maguire to Lyle and subsequently acquired by Tennent was only part (though the larger part) of
Maguire's estate; and second, that what was sold and bought – a fee
farm grant – was not the freehold of the property but technically a
leasehold, though a lease for ever. The lordship of the manor with its
rights and privileges, such as the holding of a manor court and the
obligation on all the tenants to have their corn ground at the lord's

mill, remained in the hands of the Maguires, who were thus poten-
tially in a position to annoy the new owners of the house and
demesne. With a lord of the manor as combative as Constantine, dis-
putes were almost certain to arise eventually, since the interests of
Tennent and those holding land from him and the obligations of
those same tenants as inhabitants of the manor of Inseloghagease
[Lough Eyes] were not necessarily compatible. In practice, during this
period Constantine's dire financial position and his fantasy of making
a deal of some kind with Tennent that would enable him to live in the
manor house again, made him behave more circumspectly than usual,
in Tempo at any rate.

He was less circumspect in his dealings with his mother, whose
annuity out of the estate (under the terms of her marriage settlement
of 1773) was a sore drain on his own income. Finding that she could
not depend upon regular payments, Mrs Maguire was obliged to sue
her son in the court of Chancery, where she got possession of the
property by a writ of *Habere*. This was done in Lyle's time, that is
before 1813. She then executed a lease to Lyle, in return for £64 a
year, payable out of the property he had bought from her late husband. This arrangement was interrupted by Lyle's sudden death and
legal difficulties in settling his complicated affairs. Unable to sue her
son (who was not now involved at all), she could only sue Lyle's
executors or seize and sell the property of Lyle's tenants, who in the
meantime had become tenants of his successor, William Tennent.
Cautious businessman that he was, Tennent had taken care when
buying the estate to be indemnified against such difficulties. He
would not ultimately be out of pocket, but in the meantime he was
in no particular hurry to pay. Imperious demands from the unfortunate widow begun to plague him. Mrs Maguire's lawyer in Dublin,
Fitton, wrote to explain the circumstances and to plead his client's
urgent need. Since Constantine was not involved, the lawyer thought
Tennent as possessor of the lands named as security would be obliged
to pay, and that is how things seem to have worked out. Fitton also
told him: 'Mrs Maguire and her son are not on terms, and if he even
had a right to pay the money he would not willingly pay her...'.[27]

There is also some evidence from the Tennent papers about a second suit in Chancery involving mother and son. So far as one can
gather, Constantine appears to have challenged his mother's right,
under a will, to inherit the estates of her uncle Stephen Butler's in

Tipperary and Queen's County (Laois). Butler died about 1812, but it was the end of 1816 before she got possession. One of Tennent's lawyers wrote on 1 January 1817 to tell him that Mrs Maguire had 'lately obtained a good estate, after a law suit of some standing, and in consequence of succeeding to her Uncle's property, has taken the name of Butler …'.[28] Her impatient letters to Tennent thereafter were signed 'Phoebe Maguire Butler…' – as much a repudiation of her late unfaithful husband as a tribute to her uncle. Whatever the details of the case, its outcome was a sore blow to Constantine; not only did he lose, but he was left owing more than £1,200 (say £50,000 in current values) in legal costs. In a last desperate throw, he tried to borrow from Tennent the £400 needed to initiate an appeal to the House of Lords. Tennent would not lend even this amount without the security of a mortgage on Maguire's estate – an impossible condition, because the property was already in the hands of a receiver acting on behalf of the executors of Tennent's predecessor Lyle, to whom £600 was still owing.

Constantine's solution to his difficulties was a bizarre one: he simply refused to pay his debts, preferring to go to prison, where he could live comparatively cheaply and where he would be safe from further harassment for the time being. On 3 May 1817 he was committed to Kilmainham Gaol on foot of a writ from the court of Common Pleas for the sum of £253.[29] We know nothing for certain about the plaintiff in the case beyond his name, which was H. Irvine; the only plausible person in the Dublin directory of the time is one Hezlet Irvine, a 'Manchester merchant' trading at Merchants Quay.

In view of Maguire's subsequent conduct, however, it is not at all unlikely that Irvine was playing his part in a 'friendly action'. News of the imprisonment brought a shower of writs from other creditors – foremost among them, one presumes, his lawyers. The law concerning imprisonment for debt was both patchy and complicated. A debtor could be jailed either as a result of what was called 'mesne process', whilst awaiting the outcome of a suit for seizure and sale of his property; or, alternatively, on 'final process' when his person rather than his property was proceeded against. Most cases of the second sort were settled by compromise before the debtor was actually imprisoned. Most debtors were only too anxious to avoid prison, but the law was such that someone owing a large amount and willing to put up with incarceration might force creditors to reduce their demand or even – if desperate or determined enough to take advantage of a six-year time limit in such cases – to thwart them entirely.[30] So Constantine sat out his creditors. In October 1818 he was transferred from Kilmainham to the main gaol for debtors, the Four Courts Marshalsea off Thomas Street in Dublin. There he remained for the next six years, till released in the autumn of 1824.

However determined his character, a few years earlier he might well have hesitated to take such a course. Like all the city's prisons, the Marshalsea had received a damning report from a commission of enquiry in 1808. On paper subject to a rigorous regime of inspection, headed by an inspector-general who reported to Parliament, in reality the prison authorities regularly ignored or flouted the regulations. The Marshalsea, though less than thirty years old, was a disgusting building inside. 'Debtors are the most refractory order of Prisoners', the inspector remarked, 'their rooms, staircases and lobbies are generally very filthy ...'. Notwithstanding a ban on 'spirituous liquors', large quantities were smuggled in by prisoners' friends and three rooms were let to a tapster, who rented them to prisoners at night. There were twenty-five apartments let by the marshal at a weekly rent, as well as seven common halls crammed with lodgers. A privy in one of the exercise yards was in 'a most filthy state; and what was formerly a bath was then entirely choaked up, and entirely useless'. As a result of reforms approved in 1810 the Marshalsea had been transformed by an additional exercise yard, improved lodgings and the provision of proper baths and privies. Within a short time, according to one report, 'from being a scene of filth and disorder, it had been converted into a place of comparative comfort and tranquillity...'. If the 'perfect order and cleanliness in every department' that some enthusiastic visitors detected sounds too good to be true, there had clearly been some real improvement.[31]

We have no first-hand account, from an inmate, of conditions in the Dublin prisons for debtors in the 1820s. Something of the flavour of such places, however, may be gleaned from a satirical tale (first published in 1821) featuring the Sheriff's Prison in Green Street. The book's improvident and gullible hero, Brian Boru, Esq., is lodged there when unable to pay his debts. He finds himself obliged to give the keeper three guineas a week for a small room and, as a newcomer, to treat all the inmates to large amounts of beer and whiskey in the basement Tap – an illegal commonroom-cum-shebeen for both sexes

'The Tap in Sheriff's Prison', one of the illustrations
from the 1904 edition of *Real Ireland ... by a Real Paddy* but based on an
original sketch done for the first edition (1821). The illustrations are contemporary
with Constantine Maguire's imprisonment for debt in Dublin.

and all classes where the drinks cost three times the normal price.
During the rowdy party that ensues the generous Brian is welcomed
by a song which contains these comforting words: 'Here no Bailiff
dare molest you, here no dun can show his face…'.[32] Reports of the
conduct of Constantine's reprobate brother Brian, when he was in
one of the Dublin prisons as a debtor, show that the fictional Brian's
outlandish companions were drawn from life as much as from imagination (Brian Maguire devised and ran a successful poteen still in
order to support himself in gentlemanly style).

To make imprisonment bearable, if not comfortable, Constantine
needed more money than his half pay from the army and whatever he
could get out of his estate amounted to. Despite all that had happened between them in recent years, he appears to have depended in
the first instance on his wife Frances. When Abercorn's agent
Burgoyne visited her at her home in Dublin in July 1817, he observed
that Constantine had left her penniless.

Constantine's letters to his wife, written from prison, show that he
was careful to maintain a pretence of polite normality in their relationship, though they had been living virtually separate lives for some
time. He addresses her as 'My Dear Fan' and subscribes himself 'affec-
tionately yours' or 'your affectionate C.M.' He relies on her to act as

his agent in chasing up the people dealing with his business affairs and is effusive in his thanks for her skill and success – 'I declare to God I don't know how to thank you for the part you have acted! ... I am lost in amazement ...'. He speaks of sending her to France to receive some property there for him, saying 'I have no one else to whom I could entrust such a charge ...'. When she sends him special dishes he replies with 'a thousand thanks' but adds 'I could, however, wish you would not send these things; you know it is a public mess [in prison] and we live well and very cheap'. He suggests that she should take a modest cottage in Wicklow – 'If you could procure some snug little cottage at 30 guineas per year ... the difference of exchange on your income would pay ... you would have then £400 per annum to spend as you please, and could, with any reasonable expense, educate Florry'. (This remark refers to the fact that under the terms of the Act of Union (1801) a separate Irish currency continued to exist alongside the British one. The Irish pound, based upon a shilling of thirteen pence, was worth less than the British one. Fluctuations in the exchange created opportunities for speculation, until the two exchequers were finally amalgamated in 1826.) Earlier, he had written 'I am determined more than ever to suffer martyrdom rather than leave my child a beggar'. Florry evidently visited him in the Marshalsea, for some time later he writes, 'Never send Florry here without letting me know the day before'. As we shall see, he had good reason not to welcome unannounced visits.

He even had the nerve to ask Frances if she could find some way of drawing her annuity in advance – 'if you could any way arrange some plan by which one quarter would meet another, it would be well to try it' – and to scold her when she evidently demurred at opening the subject with her former protector's grandson, the second Marquess of Abercorn. 'You ought to be candid with me in all matters of money ...', he wrote, adding, 'you ought to know that if I had an independent income, your annuity would never be named by me'.[33]

The thing that made these endearments and protestations unsavoury, once revealed, was that while extracting all he could from what remained of his marriage and his wife's income, leaving her to pay for the entire cost of Florence's upbringing and education, Constantine was spending everything he got on his mistress and his second family. Like the fictional William Dorrit in the novel by Dickens, Maguire became a long-stay resident of the Marshalsea.

During the seven and a half years he spent in prison, Eleanor Gavan lived with him. According to the evidence of the midwife who attended on these occasions, Constantine's first child by Eleanor (not counting the outcome of the pregnancy in 1814) was a daughter born in Kilmainham in 1819.[34] This child, named after her mother, was the eldest of five born during these years; the others were Hugh (1820), Elizabeth (1821), Robert (1822) and Mary Anne (1823). All were baptised in the parish of St Catherine, where the Marshalsea was located and which the register gives as the parents' abode. Two more – Philip (1825) and Catherine (1827) – were born after their parents had left prison in 1824 and had gone to live in Mountjoy Street. Robert and Catherine seem not have survived childhood, since neither is named with the rest in Constantine's will in 1832. His legal wife, meanwhile, did not know, or at least did not wish to admit that she knew, about the menage in the Marshalsea. Yet Constantine's own sisters, Elizabeth and Frances, who took the wife's part and frequently stayed with her, knew all about it and must have known too that when their brother was pleading poverty as the reason for not contributing to the support of Florence he 'continued to support a kept mistress and illegitimate children', as the barrister Wallace put it.

Eventually, however, as one of his letters from the Marshalsea reveals, this pretence had to be abandoned, whereupon Constantine upbraided Frances. 'You might', he wrote, 'have continued to visit here without meeting with any unpleasant interruptions, and your not doing so might, perhaps, be the means of visiting upon yourself the censure you wish to avoid'. Wallace's interpretation of these remarks was that during one of her visits to the prison Frances had encountered Eleanor Gavan face to face and was determined not to do so again. From then on there was no further communication between man and wife until 1830, when Frances started the suit for divorce and alimony. The judge in the ecclesiastical court described this period as 'a kind of voluntary divorce, he living in one place, and she living in another, in the same City'.[35]

5

THE AFFRAY AT DOON
AND THE HANGING
OF RUTLEDGE

THOUGH THE PRISON REGIME for Dublin debtors – or at least for those with access to cash or credit – seems to have been pretty liberal, allowing such inmates to go out during the day to conduct business (in one of his letters, Constantine proposes a meeting with Tennent at a lawyer's office in Gloucester Street), Captain Cohonny's long absence from Tempo must have made it difficult to keep a proper eye on the management of his estate there. Tenants were easily tempted to take advantage of an absent or careless landlord. Back in 1815, when negotiating with Tennent about leasing the demesne and proposing various schemes of improvement for the village, Constantine had written 'However, without you reside there little good will be done, arrange what plans we may...' and had warned Tennent of 'constant depredations' on the timber in his absence; and there is plenty of evidence in the surviving records of tenants being prosecuted for such offences. There was scope in such circumstances for tenants to pay off old scores: in 1817, a tenant named Dunn was denounced in a letter to Tennent which claimed 'he and his has completely robbed your Honours Domaine for this 4 years past'. The year 1817 was a bad one for most of the tenants, so it is not surprising to find some of them breaking the law in despair. Unrest was made worse by outbreaks of political and religious excitement in the years

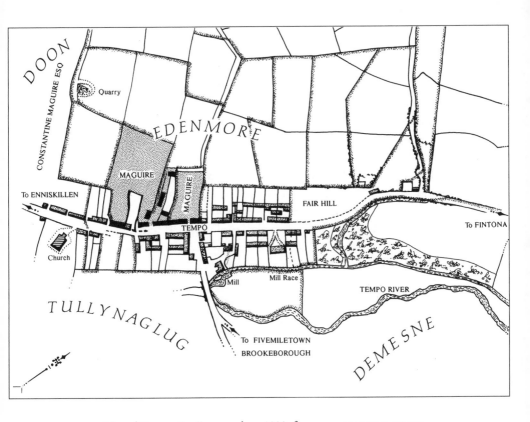

Map of Tempo, Co. Fermanagh, *c.* 1830, from a contemporary survey.
Most of the village belonged to William Tennent; the tenements still owned by
Captain Maguire were those shown with solid shading.

REDRAWN BY DEIRDRE CRONE

before and after 1820. Protestants and Catholics in and around
Tempo were evenly balanced in numbers, with extremists on both
sides organised for action or provocation in Orange and Ribbon soci-
eties respectively. Tennent's agent Leard, who was also the Church of
Ireland curate, wrote in June 1817: 'The misery and wretchedness of
the country is increased since the fair of Tempo, in which some fool-
ish & riotous ribbon men, as they are called, collected in a body on
the Common & shouted for the face of an Orangemen or Protestant.
They were opposed & dispersed by the latter; some shots were fired,
but fortunately no damage was done'.[36]

The campaign for Catholic emancipation in the 1820s, led by
Daniel O'Connell and backed by many of the parish clergy, greatly
increased sectarian feeling in Fermanagh. Father James Kelly, the
parish priest of Tempo, was attacked in the street by four men, who
were acquitted by a jury when tried. So frequent and serious were

these incidents that Tennent persuaded the authorities to establish a permanent force of the new county constabulary in the village. Disturbances of a non-sectarian kind also occurred: notices signed 'Captain Rock' appeared. These focused on the grievances of tenants from both sides concerning the operation of the manor court, in particular the fees charged by a new seneschal (presiding official) appointed by Constantine Maguire in 1822. This man, John Gibson, was also, as it happens, detested by the Orangemen because, though Protestant, his family had for many years provided lodgings for the Catholic priest. Gibson himself was assaulted and badly beaten, while his house was attacked many times. His flock of geese saved him on one such occasion, like the geese that saved ancient Rome. Leard wrote to tell Tennent that 'on Sunday night a coal was put in the stable and cow house of John Gibson, but fortunately for him his geese in the yard made a noise, & he got up & very little damage was done'. He added, however: 'I think the outrages have not been committed through any party spirit, but from dislike to Gibson alone'.[37]

Meanwhile, Constantine Maguire's prospects were improving, in some respects at least. Following a reconciliation with his mother which enabled him to raise a loan on the security of her estates in the south, which were to be his some day, he paid off some outstanding debts. After emerging from gaol, he immediately revived his enquiries about leasing the ancestral house and demesne. On a visit to Tempo in 1825, he wrote to tell Tennent that he was thinking of building a lodge there for himself but before doing so would like to have a final answer to his proposal. Nothing came of this move. Tennent's reply was that he did not intend to let the demesne to any gentleman for a residence, since he meant to have 'a residence there always open for me when circumstances may arise for retiring to that country in my old age', adding – politely if not sincerely – 'I will be happy to have you for a neighbour'.[38]

Thereafter, relations between the two of them deteriorated. The main bone of contention was the question of the quit rent of the property, as the yearly sum payable to the crown under the terms of the Ulster plantation was called. As owner of the freehold and lord of the manor, Constantine was liable for the quit rent of the whole original estate; including Tennent's portion, the sum amounted to just over £34 a year. Trouble about it was not new. In 1819, when Maguire had failed to pay it, an official called the King's Driver (acting for the Collector of Customs) had seized Tennent's cattle and put them in the village pound. Tennent's agent wrote to his employer to say that he had paid the quit rent in order to release them; the amount, almost £55 including costs, was to be reimbursed by Maguire's agent, who never seemed to have any money. In 1821 Lyle's executors, who were still collecting the income of Maguire's estate, paid the rent for that year. This was all a great nuisance, so when legislation was passed empowering the Commissioners of Woods and Forests to sell Irish crown rents, Tennent offered to buy the quit rent of Tempo. Constantine was furious. Though scarcely able to pay regularly himself, he deeply resented being displaced as nominal squire. In 1827, having come to an arrangement with his mother whereby she assigned to him 'all her right, title and interest to the Dower which she has been in receipt of out of the Estate of the late Hugh Maguire Esq.'[39], he involved Tennent in a chancery suit he was pursuing in connection with this seemingly endless saga. By the following summer relations between the two men had become so acrimonious that they actually arranged to fight a duel. *The Belfast News Letter* of 5 August 1828 included the following report:

> A hostile meeting was intended to have taken place on Friday morning last between William Tennent, Belfast, Esq., and Constantine Maguire, of Tempo, Esq., both grand jurors of the county Fermanagh. The circumstances having come to the ears of the proper authorities, they were put under an arrest, and the matter being reported to Judge Vandeleur ... his Lordship bound them in £5,000 each and 2 sureties of £1,000 each to keep the peace towards each other in the United Empire.

Tennent, in his late sixties and not given to rash behaviour, must have been sorely provoked. Duelling, particularly at that late date, was not common in the north of Ireland; it was even less common among Presbyterians, and very rare indeed among bankers of any location or religious persuasion. Maguire, in his early fifties, a military man and accustomed to shooting game for sport, would have had a distinct advantage if the encounter had taken place. In the end, it was cholera, not Constantine, that carried off Tennent; and plain murder, rather than a matter of honour, that ended the life of Maguire.

All this is by way of background to the events of 1828–29 at Tempo that were to mark an important turn in the chequered life of Captain

Cohonny. For some time a few of the bolder tenants had been taking advantage of his absence and the disturbed situation to encroach upon his land in the townland of Doon, breaking down fences and altering boundaries. They would never have dared to do so if he had regularly appeared in person, for his fierce temper was well known. Henry Leard, curate of Tempo and Tennent's land agent, telling his employer that Maguire might soon be in prison (he already was), appealed for discretion in spreading the news: '... *sed verbum sapienti*, if Mr Maguire knew that I said this much he never would forgive me, do what else he would'.[40] Perhaps the story of how the young Constantine had treated an earlier curate was in the back of Leard's mind.

Informed by his bailiff McManus of what was going on, Maguire appeared at Tempo and proceeded to take action. On 13 August 1828 he assembled a crowd of men – variously estimated at between two and three hundred – to fence and ditch his property in Doon. What followed was reported in some detail subsequently in the Enniskillen press.[41] The interface, as one might now call it, between the contending parties was the boundary between Doon and the neighbouring townland of Ratoran (part of another landowner's estate), from which a party of men with firearms advanced to attack the spadesmen as they worked. Two of Maguire's men were wounded and shots whistled past his own head when he was summoned to the front. As befitting an old soldier who had seen active service he appears to have shown coolness under fire. Noting the identity of the gunmen aiming at him he sent a messenger to Tempo to call the police, who came fairly promptly. In the meantime, when their fifteen-minute fusillade was over, the attackers were obliged to retreat, pursued by enraged workers armed with their spades, who charged down the hill towards them shouting 'Orange pups', 'Yellow Bellies' and other sectarian epithets too horrid to print. Since Maguire had both Catholics and Protestants in his employ that day, this did not go down with the latter. Maguire called back the pursuers and the marksmen made their escape. Subsequently, a well-known local Orangeman named John Rutledge was indicted for shooting at Maguire and his bailiff James McManus with intent to 'kill and murder' them; two other tenants, William Beatty (who had been evicted from a farm in Doon) and William Nixon, were charged with aiding and abetting Rutledge. All three were given good characters by their clergy (one of whom was the curate-agent Leard) and local gentry. For most people in both of these categories, politics and religion went hand in hand. Constantine Maguire was an exception, and his position at this juncture in Irish history appeared to Fermanagh loyalists to be both perverse and provocative, for though, nominally at least, a Protestant he was a Liberal in politics and a public supporter of O'Connell's campaign for Catholic emancipation. At one point in 1828 his name was canvassed by Catholic interests in the county as a possible parliamentary candidate, since before 1829 no Catholic could sit at Westminster. When he moved against the encroaching tenants on 13 August, then, what began as a landlord-tenant dispute rapidly took on the character of a sectarian affray.

The following day, Maguire wrote to a prominent Catholic barrister in Enniskillen named Randal Kernan. Kernan's brother was bishop of Clogher and both were active in the emancipation campaign. His letter ran as follows:

> A dreadful outrage took place in this neighbourhood yesterday evening. I had a number of men making fences in the mountain of Doon, above this town. About five o'clock they were attacked by a party of that loyal banditti that are for ever disturbing and destroying the peace of their country; several shots were fired by them at me and my men; one man is dangerously wounded in the thigh, another slightly in the hip, and a third had his hat struck by a slug. Two balls, intended for me, passed close to my head, and several slugs. From the deliberate aim the ruffians took it is rather surprising to me that many were not killed. I sent for the police, who, I must say, were prompt in their attendance, but having no authority to pursue or take these ruffians, they, of course, made their escape.

In a postscript he added: 'Let me have your advice. The state of this town and neighbourhood on the nights of the 11th, 12th, and 13th has been, as usual before and after orange festivals, marked with outrages and disturbances'.

Kernan replied by return of post, giving it as his opinion that Maguire's life was in danger so long as he stayed in Tempo and advising him, before he left, to lodge information about the perpetrators before a magistrate, who would then be obliged to order the police to go in search of them; he thought them guilty of a capital felony. A copy of this document should be sent to the lord lieutenant as a precaution, because, he said, several of the local magistrates were strongly identified with the Orange party. He went on:

> The proceedings of the Orangemen here [Enniskillen], on the 12th inst. (when an illegal assembly, several of whom I perceived to be armed with swords and pistols, were headed by three Magistrates and the Sub-Sheriff, and whom I saw cheered and applauded by the High Sheriff of the County and the Marquis of Ely), will, I think, in some measure, account for the daring assault made on you, which I have no hesitation … to designate an assault with intent to commit murder … it being said to be the intention of my brother, the Right Reverend Dr. Kernan, to propose you as a candidate to represent Fermanagh in Parliament at the next election is, perhaps, another cause for the outrage you have sustained.

(These letters were published in the *Dublin Evening Post*, a Tory newspaper, the following year, shortly after the triumphant climax of O'Connell's campaign, and promptly reprinted in the *Enniskillen Chronicle and Erne Packet* of 21 August 1829.)

The police duly arrested Beatty and Nixon. Rutledge escaped, however, and succeeded in getting away for North America. Approaching Newfoundland the ship in which he was travelling was wrecked in a storm. The survivors, Rutledge among them, were rescued by a vessel outward-bound for Ireland. They landed at Cork, where Rutledge's name on the passenger list attracted attention. Constantine Maguire got to hear of it. Along with his bailiff McManus he hurried to Cork, where the two of them formally identified the luckless fugitive and had him arrested. Brought under guard to Enniskillen, he was tried along with his fellow-accused at the Spring Assizes in March 1829.

The presiding judge, Baron McClelland, made little secret of his hostility to the accused. While the *Enniskillen Chronicle* for 19 March described his address to the jury as 'most luminous', the *Impartial Reporter* called his conduct 'unprecedented if not unjustified'. He hinted heavily that the jurors should do their duty as upholders of the constitution by making an example of such miscreants. In contrast, he was full of admiration for Maguire's conduct in restraining his men when they were shot at. Indeed Constantine was barely recognisable as 'a gentleman of sense and understanding, who preferred resorting to the law of his country for redress, than to suffer any hostile feeling to activate him … towards the lawless party who had wantonly formed themselves into a banditti...'. Rutledge was obliged to admit that he had indeed fired his gun but asserted unconvincingly that he had used blank cartridges, simply in order to frighten his opponents. Only one real bullet had been used, he said, in self-defence when they pursued him. The jury did not believe him, taking barely an hour to find him guilty as charged. They asked for mercy however, only to see the judge tear up their petition before he handed down the death sentence. Beatty and Nixon were acquitted.

A petition appealing for the sentence to be commuted to transportation for life was organised and presented to the lord lieutenant by the high sheriff. It attracted wide support among the Protestants of the county, including most of the gentry. When urged to add his own name, however, Maguire resolutely refused and the petition failed. Rutledge was duly hanged in front of Enniskillen gaol on 2 April. The rumour current among the more credulous of his partisan opponents was that only an effigy of the notorious Orangeman had been hanged. The remains buried in Tempo churchyard were real enough, however. The funeral was attended by a huge crowd, estimated at 4,000. Half of the mourners were identifiably Orangemen, despite the ban then in force against party processions.[42] Constantine Maguire became a pariah among many of his Protestant neighbours and, so far as we know, never visited Tempo again. Fortunately, his Tipperary inheritance came to hand at just the right time. A few years later, when he was murdered there, this disreputable story was raked up again by the Tory press. It did not escape notice that Rutledge had been condemned by Maguire to suffer the fate that he himself had avoided thirty years earlier in 1798 for a very similar offence. The contrast was made worse by the fact, frequently mentioned, that the dead man left a wife and six young children.

6

A SUIT
FOR DIVORCE AND
ALIMONY

So LONG AS CONSTANTINE remained in prison, and for five years or so thereafter when he lived in Dublin with his second family, Frances knew there was no possibility of getting any financial help from him towards the cost of rearing their daughter Florence. She had to bear all the expense herself and, unused to economy, found it hard to manage. At some point in the mid-1820s she cashed in part of her annuity in order to make ends meet. Even that was not enough, for she was obliged to take lodgers – two brothers named Sheehan – who lived with her between 1824 and 1829. In the latter year, however, old Mrs Maguire (or Maguire Butler), Constantine's mother, with whom Frances had been on good terms, at last died and Constantine succeeded to her estates in Tipperary and Queen's County. The Tipperary property, in the parish of Killaldriffe or Killardry, lay in the vale of Aherlow between the towns of Cahir and Tipperary. It consisted of the greater part of the 1,000-acre modern townland of Toureen, plus Ballymorris and Dranganmore; the denominations were differently named or had different boundaries before 1840, when the modern townlands were fixed and mapped by the Ordnance Survey. The property in Queen's County (Laois) in the parish of Ballyadams, three or four miles from the town of Athy, included the patronage of the parish, or a share of it at least, for by the early nineteenth century the right to appoint the rector alternated between the Butlers and a family named Brereton. Lewis in his

Topographical Dictionary of 1837 – that is, after the death of Constantine – noted that the right was disputed, the bishop of the diocese exercising it in the meantime. The cause of the dispute is unknown, but it is worth noting that a younger son of the Breretons, an Anglican clergyman who had been an East India Company chaplain, in 1831 married Constantine's legitimate daughter Florence – a very respectable match in the circumstances.

The acquisition of these two properties, modest as they were, transformed Constantine's income and prospects. He was even able in 1831 to buy out the quit rent of Tempo – so long disputed with Lyle and Tennent – for just under £800. More immediately, his wife Frances, Florence's mother, now thought it worthwhile to seek recompense for the expense she had had to bear alone for so many years. Early in 1830 she began a suit for divorce and alimony in the consistorial court of the diocese of Dublin. The proceedings in the trial which eventually took place there in May 1833 were the subject of the pamphlet by Dr Thomas Wallace, KC mentioned earlier. Before analysing that document (our only source of information about the case), a few words about the powers and procedures of the ecclesiastical courts may be useful.

Prior to the Whig government's reforms of 1833, the Established Church in Ireland was organised in twenty-four dioceses, four of which (Armagh, Dublin, Cashel and Tuam) were archbishoprics. Each diocese had a consistory or ecclesiastical court, which dealt with all testamentary matters (the validity and probating of wills); all matrimonial matters; cases concerning tithe (the tax that supported the Church of Ireland clergy); the administration and discipline of the Church of Ireland itself; and such things as defamation. In addition to the diocesan courts there were two others: a superior court of prerogative in Dublin (Dublin was the busiest of the diocesan courts); and – a curious survival – the court of what was called the exempt jurisdiction of Newry and Mourne, the presiding officer of which was appointed by the earl of Kilmorey, successor to the lands of the suppressed abbey of Newry. Otherwise, judges in the courts (known as vicars general) were appointed by the bishops. Appeals in disputed cases could be made from the ordinary diocesan courts to one of the four metropolitan ones; final appeal was possible beyond that to delegates in the court of Chancery. The reforms of 1833 drastically reduced the number of sees in the Church of Ireland. Among those to be extinguished when their existing holders died or retired were the archbishoprics of Cashel and Tuam.[43] The prerogative and ecclesiastical courts were subsequently investigated in 1837 by a House of Commons committee. When questioned, one of the witnesses – a solicitor who was an official of the Waterford and Lismore court – agreed that, though called a clerical or ecclesiastical court, in practice it dealt mainly with civil cases. Most of the questions asked by the committee were about the fees charged for dealing with such things as probate of wills, what professional qualifications (if any) the officers had, and how business was arranged.[44] Though somewhat diminished in their civil powers by successive reforms, the ecclesiastical courts continued to be the only courts of first resort in matrimonial matters throughout the United Kingdom until 1857, when the Matrimonial Causes Act established a new Divorce Court for England and Wales (the Act did not apply to Ireland).

Before 1857, a valid marriage could only be dissolved by a private Act of Parliament, an expensive procedure and therefore rare. To succeed, the applicant had to have already won a case against his wife in the ecclesiastical court on the grounds of her adultery, and also to have recovered damages against the adulterer in a common law suit for what was called 'criminal conversation' ('crim.con.' in lawyer's jargon). While valid marriages could be ended only by Parliament, another possibility was annulment of the marriage contract on the grounds that it had really been void from the very beginning and ought not to have taken place. If successful, this procedure bastardised any children of the marriage born in the meantime. So, had Constantine succeeded in 1816 in having his marriage to Frances Hawkins annulled, their daughter Florence would have been made illegitimate.[45]

The term 'divorce' as used in the ecclesiastical courts in the 1830s, then, did not mean what it usually means nowadays, complete dissolution of a marriage; it was what the lawyers called divorce *a mensa et thoro* (from bed and board, literally from table and bed), the equivalent of a legal separation. The courts could grant such a 'divorce' for fornication or adultery, impotency or cruelty – any gross misconduct that had made it impossible for the parties to live together. During the period of separation the court could decree that an innocent wife should be paid a maintenance allowance, called alimony, the amount of which was up to the discretion of the judge, who took into account the balance of blame and the husband's means. A woman who eloped and lived in adultery got nothing.[46]

Frances Maguire, the 'Promovent' or plaintiff in the case that was brought in 1830, sought two things: a formal divorce or separation from her husband Constantine (the 'Impugnant' or defendant) on the grounds of his adultery and cruelty, and the payment to her of a suitable sum in alimony. The proof of Constantine's long-term and continuing adultery with Eleanor Gavan was overwhelming, and defence counsel made little effort to pick holes in it. The affair, in and out of prison, the birth of numerous illegitimate children, the hypocritical conduct of the defendant and his neglect of his legitimate child were all gone over at length by the plaintiff's barrister Wallace, who presented a damning picture. The defence strategy was to ignore the case against him and instead to impugn his wife's morality, even referring to her annuity from Abercorn as 'the wages of prostitution'. Wallace had a field day with this, pointing out that Maguire had known all about the annuity before he married and had been only too keen to share in its benefits. And he added:

> If it was dishonourable to be the Mistress of any man, it was not less dishonourable knowingly to marry such a Mistress. But above all, it was and is, not dishonourable merely, but inhuman, to reproach the unfortunate person whom he voluntarily made the partner of his fortunes and fate, with the guilt or the error of which he knowingly took the profits, and made them for 27 years the provision for his family and the support of his Child![47]

While this line of attack was easily dealt with, a more serious counter-charge brought by Maguire – in fact the basis of his defence – was that his wife had committed adultery herself, and blatantly. As Wallace put it, '… he has not only endeavoured to prove that she is an adulterer since her marriage, but one who in gratifying passion has for years dismissed all sense of shame!'[48] Her counsel made some good general points in rebuttal: though lacking the protection of a husband she had secured 'as much of the countenance of the respectable part of society … as has ever been obtained by a woman who has made a first fatal step', and was far from being destitute of respectable and steady friends. It was particularly favourable to her that she merited the friendship even of her husband's own family – his mother till Phoebe's death in 1829, his two sisters up to the very beginning of the divorce suit (at which point they had been induced to alter their testimony). As visitors or inmates of her house over a long period, it was argued, they would have known if her behaviour was reprehensible. Further proof that it was not lay in the fact that her daughter Florence had been there all the time and was reared by her mother until 'respectably placed in society under her auspices' by marriage to the clergyman Brereton. No one, least of all Constantine, had ever suggested that Florence was in moral danger, as she would have been if there had been much substance in the tales related to the court by the eight witnesses the defence put forward.

These people were not, on the whole, an impressive array, and Wallace made good work of undermining what little credibility they possessed. All but one of them had at some point been employed as servants in the plaintiff's household.[49] John Byrne – described 'as a person not only very unlikely to think lightly of perjury himself, but to be a fit subject to tamper with others … a kind of aide-de-camp to Impugnant, and a drill serjeant for his witnesses …' – had only come into the service of the wife after the period of her alleged adultery and therefore could not swear to anything material. Anne Rorke, who said she was employed for five months in 1829, during the time the Sheehan brothers were lodgers, gave evidence that she had once seen Remmy Sheehan going undressed into the Promovent's bed-chamber at night, and on another occasion had seen Mrs Maguire going into his bedroom in her nightdress. She swore she had seen these things from the door of the kitchen, where she slept, but under cross-examination she had to admit that the bedroom doors could not be seen from the kitchen at all. It also transpired that she had been in the house for six weeks, not five months. To cap it all, it appeared that Sheehan had been away in England at the time of the alleged adultery. The evidence of Francis Houston, employed for a mere three weeks before leaving in disgrace, was equally unreliable. Sarah Wooten alleged that Sir William Carrol, who came on a visit, 'took a most indecent liberty with Promovent, and used the most gross familiarity, without Promovent expressing the least disapprobation'; later, the witness said she had seen him in Mrs Maguire's bedroom, by peeping through the keyhole. Carrol, an acquaintance of Frances since 1816, not only denied these allegations but also informed the court that he thought so well of her that he had introduced her to his sisters and brother, who had become her friends as well. Margaret

O'Connor, the next witness, said she had lived with Mrs Maguire in 1823 as a lady's maid. Wallace attacked her character, remarking cruelly that since then she seemed to have become more acquainted with gentlemen, in order to throw doubt on her stories about goings-on between her mistress and Remmy Sheehan. Patrick Fallon, employed for one week in 1829, swore that 'about the hour of 11 o'clock in the morning he opened a little parlour near the hall door ... and there saw the Promovent and Sheehan in the act of adultery' – this at a date when Sheehan was said to have been out of the country. Catherine Conway, who claimed to have been employed in 1823, when Mrs Maguire was living in Mount Street, vaguely described an incident involving Sheehan in which she saw him 'apparently down on one knee before Promovent, that he kept the front of his person from deponent, who came suddenly into the room, and that they (Sheehan and Promovent) seemed flurried and confused'. Under cross-examination, this cook turned out to have been 'a mere char-woman, a common wretch who worked by the day ... and who even according to her own confession, was not allowed access to the upper part of the house'. She had left the house, she said, because it was 'such an extravagant place with expensive dinners, and wines' – as Wallace remarked, surely a new reason for any cook to resign her place. The evidence of the last of the hostile witnesses, Catherine Murray, also concerned Remmy Sheehan; the adulterous intercourse between him and Mrs Maguire, it was alleged, was common talk among the servants.

Wallace, practised lawyer that he was, made a good job of exposing the inconsistencies, inaccuracies and downright falsehoods in the evidence of this dubious crew of witnesses. In a more general way, he emphasised the improbability of the conduct alleged against his client. Could she have done what she was said to have done and not only have raised her daughter to be an accomplished and respectable young woman, but also to have preserved the friendship and society of the Maguire women? Was it likely that she had been so reckless?

> Suppose Promovent to have had at the age of fifty the most violent passions of unbridled youth, and a determination to indulge them – was there no way by which private vices might be indulged in privacy? Could there have been no fit and safe opportunity found to entertain a paramour out of her own house; or in her own house with secresy by a little of the management used in such cases? [50]

The reference to her age, incidentally, is the only clue we have to the approximate date of Frances's birth: if fifty in say 1829, she was probably born sometime in the late 1770s.

The judge, who sat alone without a jury, reviewed the proceedings and the evidence on 30 May 1833. The aggrieved wife's long delay in proceeding against her husband, he said, would normally have weighed heavily against allowing the case to proceed, had the defence rested not on this technicality but on her alleged adultery. That Constantine was determined to ruin her character is strongly suggested by the following evidence. At the very end of Wallace's pamphlet is reported an intriguing exchange involving three parties – the judge (nowhere named), Sir Henry Meredith (who had opened for Mrs Maguire), and Dr Stock (Constantine's counsel). When the judge remarked that he never so much wished for a jury Meredith said 'I too wish your Honour had the assistance of a Jury, for it is my solemn conviction that there is not a Jury under heaven would have believed the evidence on the other side'. Stock's rejoinder to this was to say that the evidence had already been before a jury in a trial in the Court of Exchequer; he had a pamphlet containing a report of the trial. Meredith then said:

> I deny that the evidence was ever fairly before a Jury. In the trial alluded to by Doctor Stock, a foul and insidious attempt was made to drag this unfortunate lady before the public, by means of this evidence, when one of the parties was totally unprepared to meet it; and the trial was not, in consequence, proceeded with; and as to the pamphlet which has been referred to, I do not hesitate to call it a most atrocious Libel.[51]

One would like to be able to judge the matter for oneself, but alas no copy of this tantalising publication appears to have survived. What does appear is the likelihood that Constantine was determined to punish his wife by any means he could find.

The judge pronounced that the charge made by Mrs Maguire against her husband had been proved: the Impugnant was 'guilty of gross and shameless adultery'. The question that remained was whether she should be deprived of compensation by conduct which, he was bound to say, was provoked by the husband himself. He thought, however, that taking in the Sheehans as lodgers had been 'a very imprudent step'. Despite 'very strong' evidence to her credit, particularly from the Maguire sisters, he did not think he could say that the charges of conspiracy and perjury by Constantine's witnesses were absolutely proved. 'The Court could not ... go to the length of stamping perjury on the witnesses of the Impugnant; more particularly when it appeared there was evidence for the Promovent kept back or not brought forward'; he meant that of the two Sheehans. It is clear that Remmy Sheehan behaved very badly. Served with a writ, he promised 'to come forward and fully vindicate' Frances's character. A letter from him to her, filed in the Registry of the Court, ran as follows:

> I have read the document, it is a tissue of ill asserted [sic] falsehoods. Being on the most brotherly terms in your house may have given some colour for tempering [sic] with your servants, and distorting and prevaricating the most innocent circumstances; and I must consult a friend as to what course I ought to adopt. You have a right to my most unqualified vindication of your character, so far as I am concerned, and you shall have it fearlessly and unconditionally ... I am now obliged to go out, and shall not be back for two hours.[52]

In fact, like Captain Oates in the Antarctic snowstorm, he never returned. The judge's remark – that 'it was not to be supposed, if she [Frances] had used proper means, that he who had lived in her house for more than 5 years, and knew her conduct to be proper, would be so lost to honor, character, and manly feelings, as to decline giving his evidence, contrary to the witnesses against her' – expressed the crucial deficiency in the wife's case. He therefore dismissed it and refused to grant alimony. In doing so, he imputed no guilt to her, and added that she was at liberty to start her suit again if her husband continued 'his adulterous intercourse with Miss Gavin'.

But Frances had had enough of Ireland. So far as we know – and we know very little – she left Dublin soon afterwards and went to live with her daughter in England. Which daughter this was – Hariot, who had married an Army officer named Reed, or Florence, now married to the curate in Kent – is a mystery. We do know that the real Mrs Maguire was alive somewhere in England in the mid-1830s, but have no idea where or when she died. Her name does not appear in a list of Abercorn pensioners dated 1841, though 'Mrs Reed' and 'two Fitzjames' do. On the face of it, this suggests that she may have died sometime between 1834 and 1841. It may, however, merely mean that the legal costs of her failed case for 'divorce and alimony' had obliged her to cash in the rest of her annuity. Lawrence's controversial portrait of her in her prime was hidden away for many years, to reappear at Baronscourt only in recent times.

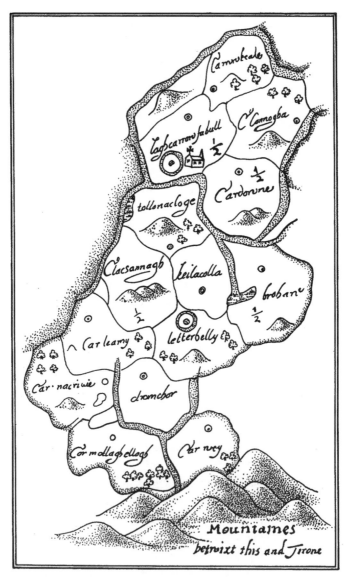

Part of County Fermanagh containing the estate granted to
Brian Maguire of Tempo by King James I.
From the map by Josias Bodley 1609

REDRAWN BY DEIRDRE CRONE

7

MURDER
IN TIPPERARY

N O LONGER WELCOME in Fermanagh, Constantine Maguire
became the resident landlord of the estate in Tipperary that he
inherited from his mother in 1829. His mother had never lived there
herself, nor had the previous owner, Stephen Butler, so there was no
obviously suitable residence for a gentleman on the property. In fact,
where exactly the Maguire family did live at Toureen is something of
a puzzle. Toureen and the other townlands that made up the estate all
lay in the parish of Killaldriffe or Killardry, which the *Parliamentary
Gazetteer* described in rather unenthusiastic terms:

> The surface lies at the entrance or expansion of the vale of the
> Aharlow, where the rivulet Aharlow, hitherto romantically pictur-
> esque, receives its voluminous affluent from the north, and moves
> away, in common-place style, to the Suir. The land, with the excep-
> tion of a small portion, is of inferior quality.[53]

The entry continues: 'The chief objects of interest are Maguire's-cas-
tle, Toureen-house, and Kilmoyler-house, – the last the seat of S.
O'Meagher, Esq.'. 'Maguire's Castle', located at the lower edge of
Toureen Wood where it runs down from the mountain towards the
banks of the river, is marked and named on the first Ordnance Survey
map of the area, published in 1840. Some ruins, possibly associated
with it, remain; and nearby is an attractive dwelling, now known as
Toureen Wood House, which, however, does not appear as such on
the first OS map. The 'Toureen House' noted by the *Gazetteer* stands

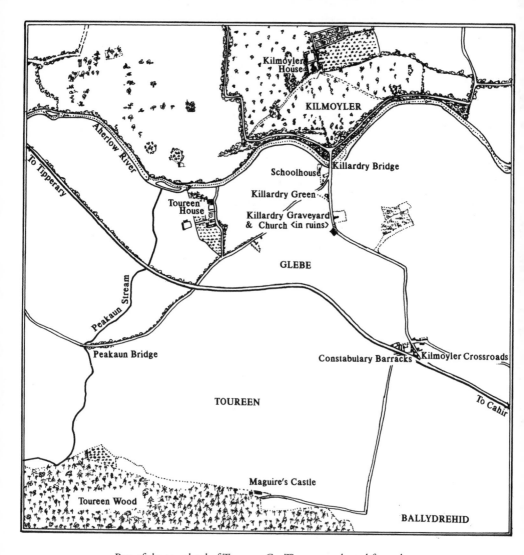

Part of the townland of Toureen, Co. Tipperary, adapted from the
1st Ordnance Survey map (1840). Kilmoyler Lodge, the scene of the murder in
1834, was situated close to Maguire's Castle.

REDRAWN BY DEIRDRE CRONE

on the level ground by the river, just across from Kilmoyler House,
which is in the townland of Kilmoyler. Both houses, with their
demesnes and gardens, are marked and named on the 1840 map.
Both of them belonged to the O'Meagher family. Described by the
OS reporters as a 'gentleman's house', Toureen House was the kind of
property that would have suited Maguire if he could find nothing
suitable on his own land, and if available and affordable. Recent ren-
ovation has revealed roof timbers dated 1836, but the house was built

more than twenty years earlier than that.

Given its imposing title, however, one might expect Constantine to have lived in the 'castle' that bore his name; the OS reports describe it as 'a habitable Castle' and 'a Castle still inhabited'. Yet it cannot have been called 'Maguire's Castle' for very long, at most only since Constantine's arrival in the district in 1829; and, though called a castle, it does not appear to have been at all imposing. One plausible guess is that the name was not only recent but quite possibly ironic, even derisive – a sly joke at an unpopular landlord's expense. Had the 'Castle' been an authentic castle, lived in by the Maguire family, it is hard to believe that it would not have been named somewhere as their residence. Yet the address of the victim given in the various accounts of Constantine's death is almost invariably Kilmoyler or Kilmoyler Lodge.

One important clue to this puzzle lies in the pages of Samuel Lewis's *Topographical Dictionary of Ireland*, the first edition of which was published in 1837 – that is, midway between the death of Constantine and the appearance of the OS map fixing the townland names and boundaries. The particular virtue of Lewis's work is that, unlike the compilers of most travel guides and gazetteers, he did not simply rely on earlier publications but instead took information from local residents, who got proofs to check before printing. The entry in Lewis for Killaldriffe lists six 'principal seats' in the parish. As well as Kilmoyler (S. O'Meagher, Esq.) and Toureen (D. O'Meagher, Esq.) these include Kilmoylermore (the late Constantine Maguire, Esq.). This place must have been Kilmoyler Lodge. If so, how? The answer is that the Ordnance Survey made considerable changes to traditional names and boundaries when fixing the townlands in their modern form. Pre-1840 Kilmoyler was much larger than the present townland of that name (which lies entirely on the northern side of the River Aherlow) and its shared ownership was indicated in the tithe records by the names 'Kilmoyler O'Meagher' and 'Kilmoyler Maguire'.[54] Toureen – Upper, Lower and Wood – was correspondingly smaller than at present. So what had been part of Kilmoyler in 1834 was part of Toureen six years later. Here, on his own land, Constantine built a lodge or cottage, possibly by adding to something already there; the term 'cottage' may have meant no more than that the house had a thatched roof. A recent survey suggests that the 'castle' nearby, not mentioned by Lewis at all, may have been a kind of summer house or folly that served to supplement the accommodation provided by a modest Lodge. The Lodge, almost certainly the place where Constantine was killed in 1834, was probably the predecessor of the present Toureen Wood House. One other source of information is relevant. By his will (1832), Constantine bequeathed to Eleanor Gavan for her life what he called 'my Cottage and Gardens, Lands and Pleasure Grounds at Toureen Wood, together with the Cow Park and grazing of said Wood ...'.[55] No other residence is mentioned. To put the location, if not the actual building, beyond further doubt, this conclusion also tallies with incidental clues in the evidence given by various witnesses in the murder trial in 1836.

The train of events that led to that trial can be traced almost entirely from newspaper reports alone; there is little first-hand evidence to be had. Fortunately Clonmel, the assize town for south Tipperary, was served in the 1830s by no fewer than three newspapers – the *Clonmel Herald*, the *Clonmel Advertiser* and the *Tipperary Free Press*.[56]

The Tory *Herald* of Wednesday 5 November 1834 announced the recent murder of Captain Maguire of Kilmoyler, whom it called 'an inoffensive gentleman who had, within a few years, come into this deeply blood-stained county to reside on his estate'. It reported that, on the previous Friday, Maguire had auctioned off corn and other goods seized for unpaid rent and had got rid of some defaulting tenants. The next morning, shortly after nine o'clock, when he had visited a 'necessary out-house' (privy), he was attacked by two men armed with muskets or blunderbusses who fired at him, then dragged him outside and smashed his skull with the butts of their weapons before running off. A magistrate had been sent for and arrived quite promptly with a party of police, who 'scoured the country but could not discover any clue to the murderous wretches'.

The rival *Advertiser*, published the same day, carried a very similar news item, though its account varied in some details and was expressed in more dramatic style. Headed 'Flagitious Murder', this too deplored having to report yet another outrage, the like of which 'may not possibly be found in the black catalogue of crime which has disgraced our county for many years'. The victim was praised as 'a gentleman of considerable property ... who possessed, in an eminent degree, every description of moral worth and excellence calculated to endear him to society'. More delicate – or less well informed – than the *Herald*, the *Advertiser* made no mention of the privy, explaining instead that 'when walking in the lawn in front of his mansion, about eight o'clock on Saturday morning last [he] was pounced upon by two miscreants who fired two shots at him and lodged their contents in his body; they also mutilated his head and other parts of his person with the butt ends of their guns'. His lady companion, who had just left him to go inside and order breakfast, rushed back when she heard the shots and 'to her indescribable dismay perceived the mangled corpse of her husband, weltering in gore'. The two papers agreed as to the likely reason for the crime, but the *Advertiser* added a reference to Maguire's recent prosecution in the 'Petit Sessions Court' of some ruffians who had damaged a young plantation on his land.

The third newspaper, the *Free Press*, founded to support the campaign for Catholic rights and its leader Daniel O'Connell, adopted a somewhat different line from the other two. The difference was reflected in the title of its report, 'Robbery and Murder of Constantine Maguire, Esq.' The writer of course condemned the 'atrocious and revolting deed, which has robbed one of the most excellent gentlemen of life, an amiable family of its natural head and protector, and society of one of its most valuable members'. What caused the author to feel 'humiliated in the extreme,' however, was to have 'our dear and suffering country scoffed at by the pensioned calumniator as the land of the bloody and atrocious murderers'.

The chief motive of the perpetrators, the *Free Press* decided, was robbery. It was said to be well known that the victim often carried large sums of money on his person; about £40 was stolen, as well as a gold watch. Not only did the paper argue a different motive, it also presented a different scenario of the crime. Ignoring what it called 'various rumours in circulation' (there is no mention of bad relations with tenants, or of the privy), it comments: 'It is thought that one of the fellows mentioned engaged his [Maguire's] attention, while the other ruffian stole from behind, and with a blow from the butt end of a blunderbuss felled him to the earth, and deprived him of his senses'. More significantly, the *Free Press* account also differed from the others in claiming that the murder was carried out silently: 'The murder was silently and promptly perpetrated – no shot was fired – no cry was heard'.

Some months later, the murder merited substantial notice in the *Annual Register*. Mainly based on the news as given by the *Clonmel Advertiser* and a Dublin publication called *Stewart's Despatch*, the

Register account settled on the ejection of defaulting tenants and the prosecution of plantation vandals as obvious motive for the crime: 'For these offences, Mr. Maguire had become obnoxious to the self-elected legislators of Ireland and consequently incurred the penalty of death'. The victim was said to have been 'walking in the lawn in front of his mansion' with his lady, who had gone to order breakfast when she heard shots and returned to find her husband dead.[57]

The Dublin Gazette of 6 November advertised an official reward of £200 'to any Person or Persons (except the Person or Persons who were principals therein) who shall, within six months ... give such Information as shall lead to the apprehension and conviction of all or any of the Persons concerned'. Two hundred pounds was the usual upper limit for rewards in such cases. No one claimed the money in this instance, at least within the time limit.

Apart from condemning the crime and its perpetrators, the immediate reaction of the Tipperary landowning establishment was to blame the authorities in Dublin for failing to include the barony of Clanwilliam (of which the parish of Killaldriffe was part) in the recent use of a new, draconian 'Act for the more effectual suppression of local disturbances and dangerous associations in Ireland'. Lord Glengall, the Cahir magnate, successfully lobbied for the extension of the coercion act, 'from his knowledge of the dreadful state of lawless and insurrectionary feeling amongst the peasantry of Tipperary'. The first consequence of not doing so, he declared, had been the murder of Maguire; the *Gazette* of 20 November announced the decision of the Privy Council to add Clanwilliam to the list.

Violence against landlords, their agents and anyone else who offended the people the *Clonmel Advertiser* called 'our midnight legislators' was a notorious fact of life in Tipperary in the 1830s. By any reckoning, the county was usually at or near the top of the list for agrarian crime.[58] The mid-thirties produced a record level of 'outrages'. In 1834, as it happens, the figures were by a wide margin the highest for any county, both in the gross number (almost 4,000) of people committed to prison and in the ratio per 1,000 of population (9.9); the ratio for the country as a whole that year was 2.8. Furthermore, Class One crimes – offences against the person with violence, such as murder – made up a larger proportion of those imprisoned and tried in Tipperary than elsewhere. Not only that, in the mid-1830s the chances of those accused of murder being found

No. 12,458.

[697]

The Dublin Gazette.

Published by Authority.

THURSDAY, NOVEMBER 6, 1834.

DUBLIN CASTLE,

November 3, 1834.

WHEREAS it has been represented to the Lord Lieutenant, that on the Night of Thursday, the 30th of October ultimo, John Carden, Esq., was fired at, while entering his own Gate, at Barnane, in the County of Tipperary:

His Excellency, for the better apprehending and bringing to justice the Perpetrators of this Outrage, is pleased hereby to offer a Reward of

ONE HUNDRED POUNDS

to any Person or Persons (except the Person or Persons who actually fired the Shot,) who shall, within Six Months from the date hereof, give such Information as shall lead to the apprehension and conviction of all, or any of the Persons concerned therein.

By His Excellency's Command,

E. J. LITTLETON.

DUBLIN CASTLE,

November 3, 1834.

WHEREAS it has been represented to the Lord Lieutenant, that on Saturday, the 1st November instant, Constantine Maguire, Esq., was Murdered in his own Lawn, at Toureen-Lodge, near Cahir, in the County of Tipperary, by two Persons unknown:

His Excellency, for the better apprehending and bringing to justice the Perpetrators of this atrocious Murder, is pleased hereby to offer a Reward of

TWO HUNDRED POUNDS

to any Person or Persons (except the Person or Persons who were the principals therein) who shall, within Six Months from the date hereof, give such Information as shall lead to the apprehension and conviction of all, or any of the Persons concerned therein.

By His Excellency's Command,

E. J. LITTLETON.

CHARITABLE BEQUEST.

THE late Richard Gillman Hawkes, of Queen-street, in the City of Cork, Wine Merchant, did by his last Will and Testament, leave, after certain Legacies therein mentioned, the residue of his Property, Plate, Furniture, Horses and Carriages, to the Rev. Mr. Lombard, and Rev. Mr. O'Callaghan, of Cork, for the sole purpose of Charity.

RICHARD BROWNE CROOKE, Executor.

To the Commissioners of Charitable
Donations and Bequests; and all
whom it may concern.

In the Matter of Michael Murphy Collier, a Bankrupt.

THE several Creditors of the Bankrupt, who have proved debts under the Commission in this Matter, are hereby required to meet the Assignee at the Office of the Agent, No. 7, Digge's-street, Dublin, on Thursday, the 13th November next, at Eleven o'Clock in the forenoon, in order to reject or receive the proposal made by Bankrupt for the purchase of the Furniture returned in his Schedule. —Dated this 30th October, 1834.

RICHARD WRIGHT, Agent to the Commission and Assignee.

Front page of the *Dublin Gazette* of 6 November 1834, offering a reward of £200 for information leading to the conviction of Maguire's murderers.

guilty appear to have been lower in Tipperary than elsewhere. For
example County Clare, which in such matters sometimes rivalled
Tipperary, in 1832 headed the number of committals with 131. Of
these, 14 were found guilty of murder and 12 of manslaughter.[59] In
that same year in Tipperary, when 120 were committed to gaol and
25 convicted, only one was found guilty of murder and executed.
Captain Cohonny, then, chose an unfortunate time and place in
which to exercise his proprietorial rights to the full, perhaps especially when he was a relative newcomer, unable to draw upon any traditional support of the kind that he would have found among at least
some of his Fermanagh kinsfolk and acquaintances.

The Irish scholar John O'Donovan, who was working at this time
for the Ordnance Survey, happened to be in Fermanagh when news
of Maguire's death became known there. In a letter dated 4 November
1834 he wrote:

> There is a report here that Constantine Maguire of Tempo was shot
> in the county of Tipperary. There was an attempt made at shooting
> him before near Tempo, but the aggressor was hanged; it is generally
> believed here that he was shot in Tipperary in revenge for the hang-
> ing of Rutledge.

So much for the reliability of general belief or what was sometimes
known in Fermanagh as 'the invoice of the country'. Two days later,
the news of the murder appeared in print in the Enniskillen papers.
Writing to his friends in Dublin again on 10 November O'Donovan
reported: 'All the old Maguires here exclaim that the Tipperary men
did not give Cohonny fair play!'[60]

Ten days later, the *Enniskillener* – a partisan Orange publication –
produced an interesting example of what is nowadays called spin-doc-
toring. On the one hand it condemned the murder, but combined
this with the assertion that such villainy was only to be expected from
Catholics, and with criticism of the victim's views and reputation.
Remarking that Maguire had chosen to live among the 'savage mon-
sters' of Tipperary, in preference to his native soil, the writer went on:

> Had this bloody deed been committed in Fermanagh, it would have
> been endeavoured to have fastened it on the Orangemen, for the
> humanity shown to poor Rutledge ... who was prosecuted with unre-
> lenting severity and, found guilty, hanged. Had this gentleman

resided in this county he would have been safe.

The paper did not fail to remind its readers that the dead man, 'murdered by Popish conspirators, was applied to to sign a memorial in favour of Rutledge' and refused.

The campaign denigrating Maguire went far beyond Fermanagh. In Tipperary the grapevine got to work almost immediately, the *Clonmel Herald* announcing:

> The female mentioned in the account of the murder of Captain Maguire ... as having witnessed the bloody deed is erroneously said to have been Mrs Maguire. The lady entitled to that name has been living with her family in England, and the party alluded to was but the *chère amie* of the deceased.

Another item in the same issue of the paper consisted of a report, reprinted from the *Wexford Conservative*, of Constantine's close shave with the law in 1798. This began, 'The late Captain Maguire was nominally a Protestant, but from his youth up professed those principles of falsely called liberalism, which have been so long a curse to the country'. According to the writer, whose information can only have come from a Fermanagh source, the young Maguire 'always evinced the most deadly hatred to the Established Church and its Ministers – so much so that in 1798 he was tried and found guilty at the Assizes of Enniskillen for setting fire to a turf stack and flax kiln, the property of the Rev. Lucas Bell, curate of Tempo'. Had the writer known that Constantine had actually been found guilty on the far more serious charge of shooting with intent to kill, his case would have been greatly strengthened. The article ended with the customary reference to Maguire's 'last and most noted act', namely his prosecution of poor Rutledge.

Yet another demolition item appeared in the *Herald* of 22 November. This one, copied from the *London Standard* and described as 'tragi-comical', began as follows: 'The murder of Mr. Constantine Maguire was committed upon a gentleman who had distinguished himself, as far as his station in life would permit, by a most boisterous support of the Roman Catholic demands; and the distinction appears to have been hereditary'. It went on to rake over an episode dating from 1780, when Constantine's father, high sheriff that year, had allegedly enraged local Protestants by letting the law take its course in the case of a young Protestant convicted on a capital charge. The lad's co-accused, all of whom were Catholics, and all much older than he, were members of a gang of robbers. It was said that they had got the boy drunk and forced him to join them. As a result of Hugh Maguire's bad example, it was argued, both Constantine and his younger brother Brian had become vociferous advocates of Catholic emancipation, despite the family's nominal Protestantism. The comical element in the article was based upon Brian Maguire's racy memoirs and his subsequent eccentric behaviour around Dublin. By 1834, however, the decayed bravo was living in destitution on the outskirts of the city, barely lasting long enough to succeed his late brother for a few months as head of the family before dying a pauper's death in 1835. Every means that came to hand, it is clear, was used to blacken the reputation of a man who in the view of his opponents must have been seen as a traitor to his religion and class.

8

'SENSATION IN COURT'
THE TRIAL OF PATRICK KEATING

IT WAS NEARLY EIGHTEEN MONTHS after the murder that some-one was at last indicted for it and brought to trial at the Spring Assizes in Clonmel, on Monday 14 March 1836, Chief Justice Doherty presiding. The inquest held on 2 November 1834, the day after the murder, had returned a verdict of 'wilful murder, by persons unknown'. All the eyewitnesses who gave evidence agreed that two men had been involved. One of them was Patrick Keating, the nephew of a tenant of the same name on Maguire's estate who had been about to be evicted for falling into arrears with his rent. According to police evidence, young Keating was twice arrested (first in January 1835) and twice released because no witness could be found to identify him in open court. Keating was taken in a third time on the night of 29 February 1836, by which date Chief Inspector Anderson of Cahir had a couple of informants prepared to identify him as one of the 'persons concerned in the murder of Capt. Maguire of Toureen Lodge'.[61] The second man, who was never appre-hended, was a mystery. Several witnesses had seen him, but all agreed that they had never seen him in the district either before or since. Two suspects were arrested on mistaken identifications and quickly released. Both perpetrators were said to have worn 'old caroline hats' and 'long raggedy coats' of a dark colour. The Second Murderer, dressed in a coat curiously described as being 'between dark and brown', had 'some dirt on his face as it were rubbed with bog mould'. Caroline hats were so called because originally made of beaver from

Carolina, a cheaper alternative to the Canadian kind. This antique style of headgear, still popular in the Irish countryside in the nineteenth century but by that date made of black felt, would have provided an element of disguise at a distance.[62]

It transpired at the trial that one witness, Maurice Fitzgerald, had seen Keating (whom he knew well) shortly before the murder along with another armed man, in the company of his uncle. Fitzgerald had made no attempt to warn Maguire that there might be danger nearby, though he must have known that the elder Keating was about to be evicted. A pre-emptive murder may have been regarded as the only sure way of stopping that eviction. The strong likelihood is that the unknown second man was a 'Ribbonman', brought in from another district to do the deed. W.S. Trench, in his racy account of life as a land agent, has a chapter entitled 'The Ribbon Code', which describes murders in the Cloughjordan area of Tipperary in 1838. In his opinion the main object of the so-called Ribbon conspiracy was 'to prevent any landlord, under any circumstances whatever, from depriving a tenant of his land'; he also describes the use of bog-mould by Ribbonmen to disguise themselves.[63]

Another witness, Michael Luddy, who had been picking crab apples in a nearby orchard, had seen the two murderers running away afterwards (he described them as 'bothered with running') and had recognised young Keating. Luddy told the court that he expected the eviction of Keating's uncle that very day and hoped to get some work out of it for himself. Robbery, which the *Free Press* implausibly advanced as the primary motive for the assault on Maguire, was certainly a secondary one. In a pre-Famine countryside hiving with people, nothing about the habits of one's neighbours escaped attention and comment. It was probably well known that the victim habitually carried on his person whatever money he happened to have. At any rate he was robbed as well as murdered. All the witnesses who were at the scene concluded that the perpetrators had found the wretched man in the privy, literally with his trousers down, had shot him there and had finished him off outside. His daughter Ellen found him 'quite dead'. Mrs Ellen Fitzgerald described him as 'lying on his side against a ditch, and about two yards from the *necessary*, his head was broken and bloody...'; his trousers were down about his feet. Mrs Maguire (Eleanor Gavan), who had run outside with her daughter and a servant girl named Margaret (Peggy) Fitzgerald, was too frightened to approach the scene closely and afterwards could remember very little about it. One of the press accounts gives the only description we have of Constantine's faithful mistress: 'In deep mourning, very respectable in appearance and like her daughter spoke well and very distinctly'.

Another eyewitness was Margaret Eager or Edgar, who had come to the house in pursuit of 'pound money', the fee for looking after cattle seized by Maguire from his tenants. Going after the Maguire women and Peggy Fitzgerald, she saw a man standing over the body. He looked at her with a kind of grin before running off. This witness explained that, being in the family way at the time, she was nervous. Hearing Mrs Maguire scream out something about firearms she became alarmed. 'In consequence of thinking there was a quarrel between Mr and Mrs Maguire, she feared the deceased might fire a shot' – a very curious observation in the circumstances but one that perhaps gives us a glimpse of Constantine's reputation in the neighbourhood and the dangerous nature that various people detected in him. Far from being the 'inoffensive gentleman' of the *Herald*'s first report – a description he would surely have despised – he was only too willing to take umbrage and not at all inclined to forgive and forget.

Peggy Fitzgerald, as reported in the *Advertiser*, though not the *Herald*, also met the grinning murderer, blunderbuss in hand, face to face. The first to reach the scene, she caused a sensation in court by her description of her master 'lying stretched dead; he opened his mouth once and died!'

Michael Luddy, the man in the orchard, who had seen both of the murderers running away and had hidden in a ditch till they passed, afterwards went to 'the great house' (as he called the Lodge) and heard the news of the murder. Only then, he said, did he realise that he must have seen the perpetrators. He did not tell the authorities until two months later, having heard that there was a reward. Of course, as he said, 'it was not for that he came forward, it was for the love of justice'. Under cross-examination he was asked, 'Did you go to Kilmoyler Lodge immediately after the murder was committed, and see the widowed wife and orphan child, and yet keep your information for two months locked up in your breast?' He could only say yes. Since giving the information that helped to bring Keating to trial, Luddy had been obliged to live in the barracks at Cashel under the protection of the police.

Intimidation of witnesses was the main obstacle in the way of bringing Keating into the dock. The most reliable of them, the servant girl Peggy Fitzgerald, had been summoned on the two earlier occasions when the accused was released. At the trial itself she explained that fear of being murdered – that the whole family might be killed even – had prevented her from speaking, until persistent pressure caused her to go by herself to the police and make a statement. Once it was known, the other members of her family – father, mother and brother Maurice – also told what they knew. Under hostile questioning, Maurice said he had gone to the police then because otherwise he 'might suffer'. It turned out that he was already known to them. He had been convicted of rape, escaping sentence only by marrying the girl (who refused to come and live with him, however).

The jury did not take long to find the prisoner guilty. He was sentenced to death and executed almost at once. Constantine Maguire thus had the rare, possibly unique, distinction among Irish landlords of having been responsible for the hanging of two of his enemies – one a Fermanagh Orangeman, the other a Tipperary Ribbonman. Had he known, it would have given him a good deal of satisfaction.

CONCLUSION

S INCE NOTHING IN THE Enniskillen newspapers suggests that he
was buried in Fermanagh with his ancestors, the likelihood is that
Constantine Maguire was buried in the old graveyard of Killardry at
Toureen. His second son by Eleanor Gavan, Philip, who inherited the
Tipperary estate, was buried there in 1901, followed by his widow in
1914. Their remains were brought from Dublin, where the family
had gone to live after selling most of the property in the 1880s. All
nine of their children were born at Toureen, however. Constantine's
elder son, Hugh, inherited the properties in Fermanagh and Queen's
County. Hugh died in 1866 leaving three sons, all of whom were
mentally unstable. When the last of them died in 1921, whatever
property rights remained to the Maguires at Tempo (head rents mostly) were inherited by one of Philip's descendants in America.
Constantine's eldest daughter by Eleanor Gavan, Ellen, whose per-
formance as a witness at the trial of Keating had made a great impression on one of the court reporters, married a Dublin surgeon in
1841.[64]

In one of his letters from Fermanagh, written shortly after the murder in Tipperary, John O'Donovan lamented the sorry fate of the
Maguires of Tempo: 'I viewed Tempo House and demesne', he wrote,
'which presents a sickening aspect; the house falling fast to ruin, the
demesne neglected, the family extinct!'[65] The downfall of such old
'Milesian' families, he mused, had been brought about by 'war,
women and madness'. Though no doubt applicable to many a family, this diagnosis may have appeared particularly apt in the case of the
Maguires, for by 'downfall' O'Donovan meant not only a fatal reduc-
tion in wealth and power but also an end to 'uninterrupted hereditary
respectability'. Constantine certainly behaved badly towards his wife
and daughter, but to his credit he appears to have been devoted to his

Ellen, and she to him. There may have been faults on both sides of the ill-fated marriage.

If the bequests listed in his will were matched by assets, for a man who had lived such a rackety life Captain Cohonny left a very respectable legacy to his companion of twenty years and their children. Eleanor Gavan was to have an annuity of £400, in addition to the house at Toureen Wood for her lifetime. Each of the three daughters was to have £800 when she reached the age of twenty-three, with interest in the meantime. Unaccustomed to responsibility, and emotionally shattered by the dreadful circumstances of her lover's murder, Ellen Gavan seems to have gone to pieces. Though named in the will as the children's guardian and sole executrix, she was unable to act properly in either role. A note added to the probated copy of the will tells us that 'having been duly cited to accept or refuse the burden of the execution thereof and she having in no wise appeared thereto', she had been replaced as administrator of the estate by an unmarried woman (a Gavan relative?) with an address in Russell Street, Dublin. Miss Lucy Stapleton is described also as the guardian of the older boy. The two boys were to have sums of £50 a year each for their education and support, rising to £80 at age eighteen; and their trustees were empowered to spend up to £500 on each of them 'to advance them in trade, business or profession' (the elder, Hugh, trained as a lawyer). At probate, however, Constantine's 'effects' (personal possessions) were sworn as 'under £780', so perhaps he was guilty – not for the first time – of wishful thinking.

Nevertheless, he had managed to achieve, for the first time in his life, something like financial solvency and evidently looked forward with some confidence to the future. In this will he instructed the family trustees not to permit any cutting of his new plantations at Toureen before 1 January 1865; the money from the sale of the timber thereafter was to be 'laid out in the purchase of lands held in fee, fee farm or lands renewable for ever'. In the long run, political developments in Ireland were to undermine this plan for restoring the family's standing as landowners. All the same, the Maguires of Tempo managed in some fashion to hang on to their Fermanagh estate for the whole period from the Plantation to the Land Purchase Acts. Even now a few nominal ground-rents there remain, not worth buying out but scarcely worth collecting. Apart from that, the lordship of the manor of Inseloghagease may perhaps still be a ghostly presence, somewhere in that legal limbo to which are consigned things that have no practical existence (the manor court at Tempo died out years before such courts were officially abolished in 1859) but which have never been formally transferred or extinguished.

At one level, the story of Captain Cohonny's chequered life and brutal death is interesting simply as human drama. Since it is set in the past, however, no historian can be content to let the curtain come down without an epilogue of some sort commenting on its interest as history. In this respect, the first point to make is that telling the tale adds something to our knowledge of the local history of Fermanagh and Tipperary. Secondly, though in general an obscure minor figure, Maguire was not a stock character but differed significantly from the stereotype Protestant landowner of his time. This fact, along with Tipperary's reputation for rural mayhem, made his fate a subject of comment and controversy far beyond his immediate circle, as the entry in the *Annual Register* and newspaper reports show. Thirdly, while his rather undistinguished military career tells us little or nothing about the officer class of the French war period, his sudden acquisition of a commission in the Army early in 1799 neatly illustrates the swift change of allegiance that characterised a good many United Irish sympathisers in the aftermath of 1798.

No less valuable, perhaps, is the insight we are given into the world of shabby gentility that Constantine inhabited for most of his life, a world above all insecure and debt-ridden, haunted by creditors and desperate legal manoeuvres, dependent for improvement on the vagaries of inheritance or the lottery of a favourable verdict in Chancery. Such an outcome might suddenly make a man proprietor of land in a strange county and, if choosing to live there, a stranger in his native place. What W.S. Trench called the 'realities of Irish life' for one such combative landowner were brought into sharp focus at Kilmoyler in 1834. No less interesting, though more oblique, are the glimpses of the realities of life for a selection of otherwise invisible local people – farmers, labourers, servants – as they emerge, hesitant or bold, into the limelight of a trial for murder in which their evidence may cause a neighbour to be found guilty and hanged in public.

The last word must be about Constantine Maguire himself, the author or abettor of many of his own misfortunes. On the evidence available to us, it is difficult to admire him. There is no doubting either his physical courage or his mental energy, he was both intelligent and well educated – probably at Portora Royal School in Enniskillen, though no enrolment or attendance records earlier than the 1850s have survived to confirm this – and he could evidently be charming when he wished. On the debit side, he was also hot-tempered, arrogant and unforgiving, a man to make enemies and keep them. Personality and temperament apart, he appears to have been driven by two related forces. One was the intense and lasting disappointment he felt at the loss of most of his ancestral inheritance; he longed to return to the old house and demesne at Tempo. The other was an absolute determination, by whatever means came to hand, to maintain his status as a member of the landed gentry. A third factor, which somewhat cut across this resolve, was his marriage to Frances Hawkins – to begin with, one of the means that came to hand; later, after he took up with Eleanor Gavan, more of an obstacle to his plans. In the circumstances, his devotion to Eleanor can be seen as a romantic passion, a reckless risking of his life's main aim, and therefore in its way admirable. On the other hand, his rejection of Frances and their daughter Florence appears to have been remarkably ruthless and vindictive, not admirable at all.

Though not an edifying tale, then, the story of Captain Cohonny gives us some revealing glimpses into an obscure province of that foreign country we call the past.

NOTES

1 C.J. Woods (ed.), *Journals and Memoirs of Thomas Russell, 1791–5* (Dublin: Irish Academic Press, 1991), p. 75.

2 Lyle to Tennent, 25 July 1813 (Emerson-Tennent papers, Public Record Office of Northern Ireland, D.2922/H/3/6).

3 Fermanagh Grand Jury Bill Book, 1792–1861, record of Lent Assizes, 1798 (PRONI, FER/4/8/1).

4 *Journal of the House of Commons of the Kingdom of Ireland*, vol. 18 (1799), Appendix, cclxxxviii; 'Extract of a letter from Enniskillen dated July 28', *Belfast News Letter*, 3 August 1798.

5 O'Donovan's letter is dated 10 Nov. 1834. See John B. Cunningham (ed.), *John O'Donovan's Letters from County Fermanagh* (1834) (Belleek: St Davog's Press, 1993), p. 63; hereafter cited as *Letters*.

6 For the history of the Maguires of Tempo during the seventeenth and eighteenth centuries, see W.A. Maguire, 'The Lands of the Maguires of Tempo in the Seventeenth Century', *Clogher Record*, vol. XII, no. 3 (1987); 'The estate of Cú Chonnacht Maguire of Tempo: a case study from the Williamite land settlement', *Irish Historical Studies*, vol. XXVII, no. 106 (1990); and 'Castle Nugent and Castle Rackrent: Fact and Fiction in Maria Edgeworth', *Eighteenth-Century Ireland*, vol. XI (1996).

7 For what follows, see Anselm Faulkner, 'The right of patronage of the Maguires of Tempo', *Clogher Record*, vol. IX (1976–8), pp. 167–86.

8 'Services of Officers on Half-Pay, 1828' (War Office papers, PRO London, WO 25/767). Henry Manners Chichester and George Burges-Short, *The Records and Badges of every Regiment and Corps in the British Army* (London: Wm Clowes & Sons, 1895), pp. 468–70.

9 *Dictionary of National Biography*, entry for Baird; (Sir) Robert Wilson, *History of the British Expedition to Egypt* (London, 1802).

As an officer of the 88th Foot, Maguire must have qualified for two medals for the Egyptian campaign. The East India Company awarded its Egypt medal in gold to General Baird and fifteen of his senior officers; 2,199 junior officers and other ranks received a silver version. Secondly, the nominal overlord of Egypt, the Ottoman sultan Selim III, awarded the Order of the Crescent to officers and NCOs – gold medals to officers, silver to NCOs. (Ll. Gordon, *British Battles and Medals* (London: Spink & Son, 1971, p. 17).

10 'Services of Officers on Half-Pay, 1828'. We know little about the details of Maguire's work in the Recruiting Department because its archives were destroyed in a fire at the Tower of London in the 1840s.

11 *Memoirs of Brian Maguire, Esq., late an officer in the Hon. East-India Company's Native Army in Bombay* (Dublin: W. Cox, 1811).

12 National Library of Ireland, Genealogical Office MS 179.

13 G.E.C.[ockayne], *The Complete Peerage*, 12 vols (London, 1910), vol. 1.

14 Lady Mary Baillie-Hamilton, 'John James, 1st Marquess of Abercorn, K.G.', unpublished typescript, c.1904 (Abercorn papers, PRONI, D.2152/2). A.P.W. Malcomson, 'A lost natural leader: John James Hamilton, first marquess of Abercorn (1756–1818)', *Proceedings of the Royal Irish Academy*, vol. 88, C, no.4 (1988), pp. 66–70. Abercorn's friend William Pitt the Younger, who had

advanced him two steps in the British peerage by having him made a marquess, balked at his request to be made a duke and could not see his way to appoint him lord lieutenant of Ireland either. The two were estranged for many years.

15 G.W.E. Russell, *Collections and Recollections* (London: T. Nelson, 1898); Mary Baillie-Hamilton, 'Abercorn', pp. 3, 48, 80, 82.

16 *A Report of the Proceedings in the Consistorial Court, Dublin, had on the 4th of May, 1833... in a suit for Divorce and Alimony, instituted by Mrs. Frances Augusta Maguire, against Constantine Maguire, Esq., for Adultery, etc. together with the Sentence of the Court, etc.* (Dublin: Richard Milliken & Sons, 1833); hereafter cited as *Report of the Proceedings*.

17 Hawkins to Abercorn, undated (Abercorn papers, PRONI, D.623/A/234/13).

18 Kathryn Cave (ed.), *The Diary of Joseph Farington*, vol. VII January 1805–June 1806 (Yale: Yale University Press, 1982), pp. 2516, 2527, 2750.

Lawrence's portrait of Mrs Hawkins cost £50. When exhibited in 1806 it was entitled 'A Fancy Group'. A version of it, engraved by W. Gillet, was published in 1846 with the sentimental title 'The Faithful Friend' (presumably the dog). See Kenneth Garlick, *Sir Thomas Lawrence* (London: Routledge & Kegan Paul, 1954).

19 Mary Baillie-Hamilton, 'Abercorn', p. 90.

20 Hamilton to Abercorn, 24 Sept. 1803 (Abercorn papers, PRONI, D.623/A/95/18). See also references to Mrs Hawkins in J.H. Gebbie (ed.), *An Introduction to the Abercorn Letters* (Omagh: Strule Press, 1972).

21 Burgoyne to Abercorn, 12 May 1807 (Abercorn papers, PRONI, D.623/A/122/20). Luke Gardiner, second Viscount Mountjoy (later earl of Blessington) was one of a coterie of hard-drinking and loose-living society men in the Strabane area at this period; his brother-in-law, the Rev. Robert Fowler (incumbent of the parish that included Baronscourt) was another. Pitt had promised that, when vacancies arose, Abercorn should be allowed to nominate the next Irish representative peer and the next Irish bishop. When (after Pitt's death) the nominees proposed turned out to be Mountjoy and Fowler, the then chief secretary of Ireland – Sir Arthur Wellesley, later Duke of Wellington – bluntly told the prime minister, Lord Liverpool, that neither man was fit to be apppointed (Malcomson, 'A lost natural leader').

22 Hamilton to Abercorn, 1 June 1807 (Abercorn papers, PRONI, D.623/A/98/24).

The fate of the child born on the night of the marriage ceremony is unknown. Presumably it died in infancy, for Abercorn acknowledged his sons and provided annuities for the survivors in his will (1809). A codicil refers to the baptism of two Fitzjames boys in London in 1811, one aged two years, the other two months. Neither could have been born in 1807. The register of St James's Piccadilly for 27 April 1811 shows that these boys were the sons of 'James John Fitz-James' and 'Phebe' – the form used for husband and wife throughout the record. Curiously, however, information in the columns headed 'Born' and 'Baptised' has at some point been not just erased or stroked out but entirely obliterated by scraping off the whole top surface of the paper. We have no idea who Phebe was (Register of baptisms, 1811, for St James, City of Westminster Archives).

23 *Report of the Proceedings*, p. 8. Constantine Maguire had family connections in west Tyrone. Sir John Stewart Hamilton of Donemana, a kinsman of the Abercorns and through their influence for many years MP for the borough of

Strabane, had married as his third wife Susanna Maguire, a daughter of Philip Maguire of Tempo and an aunt of Constantine; she died sometime before 1787. Hamilton had a robust sense of humour. At an official reception, soon after this sad event, the Duke of Rutland (Lord Lieutenant 1784–87) sought to put the backwoodsman at his ease by remarking on the prospects of a good harvest because recent rain would soon bring everything above ground. 'God forbid!', replied Hamilton, 'for I have three wives under it' (E. Johnston-Liik, *History of the Irish Parliament, 1692–1800*, 6 vols (Belfast: Ulster Historical Foundation, 2002), vol. 4, p. 348).

24 Hamilton to Abercorn, 14 June 1807 (Abercorn papers, PRONI, D.623/A/97/50, 56).

25 *Report of the Proceedings*, p. 16.

26 Burgoyne to Abercorn, 24 July, 2 Aug., 16 Aug., 26 Sept., 22 Oct. 1816; 22 July 1817 (Abercorn papers, PRONI, D.623/A/129/17, 19, 21, 27, 33; and A/130/37).

Aaron Arrowsmith (1750–1823) was a fashionable maker and publisher of maps who worked in London from 1770. His output included maps of Scotland and South India, as well as Ireland (*DNB*). For the context to annulment suits, and a case study of a notable example of the same period as Maguire's attempt, see W.A. Maguire, *Living like a Lord: The Second Marquis of Donegall, 1769–1844* (Belfast: Appletree Press, 1984), pp. 62–75.

27 Fitton to Tennent, 18 July 1817 (Emerson-Tennent papers, PRONI, D.2922/H/6/12). William Tennent's accounts for the years 1817–23 show half-yearly payments of £32 to Mrs Maguire Butler.

28 Tisdall to Tennent, 1 Jan. 1817 (Emerson-Tennent papers, PRONI, D.2922/H/6/6).

29 Kilmainham Gaol Register, 1815–23 (National Archives, V16–6–38).

30 See James Kelly, 'The conditions of debtors and insolvents in eighteenth-century Dublin', in David Dickson (ed.), *The Gorgeous Mask: Dublin 1700–1850* (Dublin: Trinity History Workshop, 1987), pp. 98–120.

31 *Journal of the House of Commons*, vol. 63 (1808), Appendix 50; J. Warburton, J. Whitelaw and R. Walsh, *History of the City of Dublin*, 2 vols (London: Cadell & Davies, 1818), vol. 2, pp. 1055–58.

The original Marshalsea was a court held before an English royal official called the knight marshal. His office was the marshalcy, hence the name of the prison in Southwark in which he confined debtors and, by extension, similar prisons elsewhere. The one in Southwark, so vividly described by Dickens in *Little Dorrit*, was abolished in 1842, and the office itself in 1849.

32 [Pierce Egan], *Real Life in Ireland... by a Real Paddy* (London: Methuen, 1904), pp. 192–200. Four editions were published between 1821 and 1829.

33 *Report of the Proceedings*, p. 22.

34 *Report of the Proceedings*, pp. 12–13.

35 *Report of the Proceedings*, p. 54.

36 Leard to Tennent, 27 June 1817 (Emerson-Tennent papers, PRONI, D.2922/H/18/48). See W.A. Maguire, 'Banker and Absentee Landowner', *Clogher Record*, vol. XIV, no. 3 (1993), pp. 7–28.

37 W.A. Maguire, 'Banker and Absentee Landowner'. See also J.E. McKenna, *Diocese of Clogher Parochial Records*, 2 vols. (Enniskillen, 1920), vol. 2,

p. 266; and Peadar Livingstone, *The Fermanagh Story* (Enniskillen: Cumann Seanchais Chlochair, 1969), pp. 158–66.

38 Tennent to Maguire (draft), 13 Sept. 1825 (Emerson-Tennent papers, PRONI, D2922/H/3/84).

39 Maguire to Tennent, 26 Oct. 1827 (Emerson-Tennent papers, PRONI, D.2922/H/6/25).

40 See W.A. Maguire, 'Banker and Absentee Landowner', p. 13.

41 *The Enniskillener, The Enniskillen Chronicle and Erne Packet* and *The Impartial Reporter*. I am indebted to Margaret Kane, Enniskillen Library, for her help in searching the files. See also Livingstone, *Fermanagh Story*, pp. 155–9.

42 W.C. Trimble, *History of Enniskillen*, 3 vols (Enniskillen: *Impartial Reporter*, 1920), vol. 3, pp. 871–2.

43 R.B. McDowell, *The Irish Administration, 1801–1914* (London: Routledge & Kegan Paul, 1964), pp. 118–19. The abolished sees were amalgamated with those that remained. Not until 1864, however, was the number of church courts also reduced to a dozen.

44 *Report from the select committee appointed to enquire into the state of the prerogative and ecclesiastical courts in Ireland*, H.C. 1837 (412), vi.

45 A.H. Manchester, *A Modern Legal History of England and Wales, 1750–1950* (London: Butterworth, 1980), pp. 375–6.

46 Manchester, *Modern Legal History*, p. 375.

47 *Report of the Proceedings*, p. 9.

48 *Report of the Proceedings*, p. 10.

49 *Report of the Proceedings*, pp. 32–47.

50 *Report of the Proceedings*, p. 48.

51 *Report of the Proceedings*, pp. 60–1.

52 *Report of the Proceedings*, p. 49, footnote.

53 *Parliamentary Gazetteer of Ireland* (Dublin, 1844), under Killaldriffe.

54 Tithe Applotment Book for the parish of Killaldriffe, 1834 (National Archives, Dublin, TAB 27S/31).

55 Last will and testament of Constantine Maguire 'of Tempoe in the County of Fermanagh, Esquire', 1 Sept. 1832 (National Archives, T. 9832a, 1835).

56 Files of *Clonmel Advertiser, Clonmel Herald* and *Tipperary Free Press* for 1834 and 1836 (National Library of Ireland), with thanks to Justin Martin for his help with the search.

57 *The Annual Register ... of the year 1834* (London: Rivingtons, 1835), p. 169. The date of the murder is wrongly given as 24 October instead of 1 November.

58 *Returns from clerks of the crown ... of the several counties etc. in Ireland, of the number of persons committed to the gaols, 1834*. HC 1835 (295), xlv, 269.

In the 1870s, one Tipperary estate was notable for giving leases with a covenant making the lease void if the tenant or any of his family committed a murder (W.E. Vaughan, *Landlords and Tenants in Mid-Victorian Ireland*. Oxford: Oxford University Press, 1994, p. 108n.).

59 *Returns from clerks of the crown ... of the number of persons committed ... for trial in the year 1832*, HC 1833 (61), xxix, 89.

60 *Letters*, p. 54.

61 Outrage Reports, Co. Tipperary, 1836. Letter of 2 Mar. 1836 (National Archives, Dublin, CSORP-OR 1836, letters dated 30 Jan. 1836 (27/51), 21 Feb. 1836 (27/78), 2 Mar. 1836 (27/97).

62 Caroline or Carolina beaver hats were usually worn by servants in the eighteenth century. The cheaper felt kind survived in some rural areas of Ireland into the later nineteenth century.

63 W. Steuart Trench, *Realities of Irish Life* (London: Longmans, Green & Co., 1868), pp. 48, 51. Trench uses the terms 'Ribbonmen' and 'Ribbon Society' very loosely to mean rural agitators of any sort throughout Ireland. Strictly speaking, however, the Ribbonmen were a largely northern manifestation of resistance to authority – such as the men who threatened to murder Trench in Co. Monaghan in the 1850s.

64 Ellen Maguire's marriage, to William Henry Suffield, MD, of Clifden, Co. Galway, took place on 1 June 1841 in St George's Church, Dublin (marriage register, RCB Library, Dublin).

65 *Letters*, pp. 69–70.